Freedoms to Share

Methodist Prayer Handbook 2016/2

Roger Walton

Rachel Lampard

In January 1941, when the United States President, Franklin D Roosevelt, delivered his State of the Union address, much of western Europe was occupied by Nazi Germany. In the midst of war, he spoke of a vision of a future founded upon four essential human freedoms: of speech, of worship, from want or poverty, from fear.

These universal freedoms were depicted in four paintings by Norman Rockwell: the worker speaking out unafraid; the devout woman lost in prayer; the family sharing a Thanksgiving meal; and the parents tucking children into bed. So many people do not share in such freedoms. Today they will fear the knock on the door, struggle to feed their children, seek shelter from the falling bombs.

A lack of freedom takes other insidious forms too; people find themselves bound or enslaved by abusive relationships, racism, addiction, materialism, individualism, selfishness or sin.

The cry for freedom is both personal and universal – and is a cry which is heard and echoed in Christ. The freedoms which Jesus longs for us to have are not just heavenly aspirations. In the prayer which he taught his disciples he said, "Your kingdom come, your will be done, on earth as it is in heaven."

Jesus broke forever the barrier between God's will on earth and heaven, and lets God's freedoms flood into the messy, war-torn, unhappy corners of our world. What a challenge we have then, to share those freedoms, the personal and the universal, as God's kingdom comes on earth as it is in heaven!

Roger Walton, President and Rachel Lampard, Vice-President, British Methodist Conference 2016/2017

Chair
Inderjit Bhogal
David Friswell
Andy Jackson
Ken Kingston
Primavera Quantrill, Editor

Editing and typesetting
Primavera Quantrill
Peter Quantrill

Freedoms to Share

Uplifted in praise, O God,
are the hands of Mary, Mother of the Lord,
raised to magnify your glory,
exulting in the justice of your reign,
rejoicing in the gift of your salvation.

Uplifted in sacrifice, O God,
are the hands of your Son,
our Saviour Christ,
raised in resurrection light,
imprinted with the wounds of love,
interceding for the captive ones.

Uplifted in hope, O God,
are these hands of mine,
raised in prayer to you,
longing for the light of your presence,
awaiting the gifts of your grace,
seeking the freedom
of your boundless love.

Norman Wallwork, Chair,
Methodist Prayer Handbook Committee

Lord, you have given us freedom.
By your sacrifice you have set us free
to love and serve you with all our hearts,
no longer bound by the constraints
of modern society.
Such freedom is a joy.
Help us to do all we can
to share it with those whom we meet
and bring them to love you too. Amen.

Margaret Bickerdike, Bexhill-on-Sea

The inner 'no'

Please help me remember that sometimes
I need to say an inner 'no':
to stress,
to invaded boundaries,
to aggression.
To turn my head away, to break eye contact.
Sometimes it's okay to withdraw
and to be silent. Amen.

Fiona Marshall, writer, London

Liberating God, you come to us as we are:
enslaved in selfishness and self-interests;
imprisoned in prejudices and pride;
trapped in long-established habits of resistance to change and growth.
You come to us, to set us free in Christ.
You meet us in your grace and you melt us by your love.
You call out what and who we might be.
Release us, this day, freely to live holy and just lives.
And empower us with your freedom, so that all our words and actions
may point to your redeeming love and glorify your name. Amen.

Roger Walton, President, British Methodist Conference, 2016/2017

Dear Lord, bless all the people in the middle of wars and protect them from harm.
Help the persecutors see what they are doing and make them stop.
We thank you for all that you have done for us. Amen.

Cameron Fleming-Fido, Year 5, Boughton-under-Blean and Dunkirk Methodist Primary School

(Bob Faraway)

Anthems of freedom,
echoes in every heart,
aches in all creation.
Call and challenge in all life,
celebrate every minute.
Knocked down, I rise again.
Bound and bloodied in oppressive chains,
I refuse to bow.

Dance in freedom,
creation shows how.
Clap with every flap and wave.
Rise above barbarity and barbed wire.
The blood of Christ makes me whole.
The body of Christ makes me free.
With freedoms to share,
held in hands of love and prayer,
the light and life of God beckons me on.

Inderjit Bhogal, Learning and Development Officer (Ministry Development), Bristol and West Midlands

Loving God, you have generously given us all such freedom;
we ask that you help us to use this freedom wisely:
to love others more than we love ourselves,
to care for others more than we care for ourselves,
and to be more selfless than selfish.
And, in expressing our freedom in these ways, may we encourage others to do likewise.
In the loving name of our Saviour and Lord, Jesus Christ. Amen.

Wendy Brown, West Hertfordshire and Borders Circuit

As you free us, Lord God, from slavery to self and sin,
show us how to set others free from their enslavements.

May we be liberators:
for the prisoners of fear,
for those held fast by addictions,
for those trapped in poverty and poor housing, and
for all for whom disability imposes restrictions in everyday living.

Help us to surrender ourselves, to be part of the answer to these prayers, giving care, compassion and time to others, as to you. Amen.

Stephen Bales, supernumerary minister, West Penwith Circuit

I will not eat my bread alone
(Maggie Patchett)

When I hear the persistent cry,
"Big Issue, please," and then pass by,
help me daily to declare
I will not eat my bread alone.

When I see on the TV screen
staring eyes and bodies lean,
help me daily to declare
I will not eat my bread alone.

Empty words would I not speak
but with each sacrifice entreat,
help me daily to declare
I will not eat my bread alone.

For your love will be reborn
when none is empty or forlorn,
help us daily to prepare
that none need ever eat alone.
Based on Isaiah 58:7

Vivien Firth,
supernumerary minister, York Circuit

In a world that watches as the vulnerable ache, grant us wisdom.
In a world that stands by helplessly as children die, grant us a profound conscience.
In a world where needs cannot be met or fed or nourished, grant us righteous anger.
May we take our responsibility for the weak seriously,
may we stand, attentive, by the disadvantaged
and may we feel obligation, as to our own family, to those who are suffering.
And in our God-expectant hope, may we act justly, love kindness
and walk humbly with you, our God. Amen.

Andrea Sheppick, local preacher, Shropshire and Marches Circuit

Lord, we all have possessions, many of which are dear to us.
Often, even when we know we have enough, we are eager to have a little more.
Help us to think of those in dire poverty;
not only overseas, but in our own country, in our own communities.
Lord of all goodness,
we pray that you will help us to give gladly from the store we have, whether great or small,
to forgo the possession we may desire but do not need,
to enable those who have little or nothing to receive the basic needs to live.
We ask you to help us not to be selfish and always be willing to share. Amen.

Michael Limmer, retired bookseller, Witney

Loving God, help us to respond willingly to the prompting of the Holy Spirit:
open our ears that we may listen to your voice;
open our minds that we may understand your word;
open our hearts that we may share your love.
This we ask through our Lord and saviour, Jesus Christ. Amen.

Coral Ryalls, local preacher, Yeovil and Blackmore Vale Circuit

Lord, when I switch on my radio today, help me to understand some of the ways that you are at work here in your world, and lead me to discover whether there is any way that I can share in what you are doing... but help me always to remember that you are the one in charge, not me. Amen.

Tony New, New River Circuit

Open our ears (Carolyn Lawrence)

Lord God, we commit ourselves to you.
Be with us at our times of greatest need,
meet us on our journey and send us on our way,
renewed in your love and power,
rejoicing in hope,
giving ourselves in service to you through others,
willing to be changed by you,
and becoming more like you each day. Amen.

Patricia Batstone, local preacher, Mid-Derbyshire Circuit

Lord God, we are called to love you with all our heart and soul and strength and mind.
Give us pure hearts so that in the encounter with others we always see you.
Fill our souls with delight in your love that we might share it with everyone we meet.
Help us to be strong in the face of discouragement or difficulty
so that even then we may feel your presence with us.
Open our minds to new ideas and possibilities so that your will be done, not ours. Amen

Jane Bingham, Learning and Development Coordinator, East Central Region

Alleluia! We offer praise to the God who loves us.
We ask God's blessing on all who work: in the fields or factories,
or in offices, or shops, on the sea; to provide for our needs.
Alleluia! We serve a risen Lord who is sufficient for all our needs and desires.
It is amazing how the Holy Spirit enables us to work together and empowers us
to worship and praise our God and share all this with others. Amen.

John Cowan, lay minister, Birmingham (West) and Oldbury Circuit

Prayer of thanks for the essentials
Dear Lord, in our world of plenty we forget to
thank you for the things we really need:
  thank you for the food that keeps us alive;
  thank you for clean water to drink;
  thank you for the roofs above our heads;
  thank you for our health;
and thank you for your Son.
You give us far more than we need.
Let us not be corrupted by the riches of the world,
but share our wealth with others
and store up our treasure in heaven.
In Jesus' name. Amen.

Greg Sargent, local preacher, West Norfolk Circuit

You reveal your love for us
(© Anya Goldsack, used with permission)

Lord Jesus, you are the source of all that is good,
all that is joyful
and all that is loving,
and we thank you for each and every way in which you show yourself to us;
for your presence in the small things, as well as the great and magnificent:
the comforting touch of a friend's hand,
the warmth of genuine welcome, a human smile or the wag of a dog's tail.
In so many ways, Lord, you reveal your love for us.
Help us to see and truly understand that you want us as your friends
and that, as we open our hearts and minds to you,
you will always be there to welcome us into yours.
For this we are truly grateful. Amen.

Ren, Christian Poet

We ask God's forgiveness for missed opportunities and for our unwillingness to make major adjustments to our lives to join in what God is doing. We pray that we will hear the call loud and clear and become involved in the work of the kingdom. Amen.

John Sweeney,
former North West District Superintendent,
Methodist Church in Ireland

Almighty God, Father,
blinded by my sin, I cry out to you:
have mercy on me.
Lord Jesus, light of the world,
pierce my heart of darkness with your love.
Spirit of God, comforter,
let ears deafened by this world
receive your peace. Amen.

Daniel Pratt Morris-Chapman,
mission partner, Italy

Gracious God, in the call to be your disciples we hear your call to fullness of life,
marked by love and care for self and neighbour,
where true community crosses every barrier.
Forgive us for the times we have been prepared to accept
second best for ourselves and others,
and allowed division and inequality to separate people from one another and from you.
Among the many voices calling for our attention, help us discern what is life-giving,
and give us the courage and determination to take up your way of life. Amen.

David Bush, General Secretary, Methodist Church of New Zealand

God of love, we know that all is not right in your world.
We concentrate on what is broken, and not on how it might be mended.
We criticise often and praise little; we see the darkness and not the glimmers of light.
We are jealous of our own freedoms, and trample on the freedom of others.
We look to ourselves and not to you.
Forgive us and turn us around, Lord, that we might see possibilities:
hope, promise, grace, healing and love. In the name of Jesus. Amen.

Connie Jeffery, local preacher, Thames Valley Circuit

The kingdom of God has no favouritism
Dear Lord, thank you for loving us even though we are all different.
Thank you for forgiving us when we have done something wrong.
Thank you for helping us to get it right. Amen.

Jasmine Sawyer, Year 4, Westleigh Methodist Primary School, Leigh, Lancashire

Thank you, Lord, for Christmas and birthdays. I love celebrating things. Amen.

Owen Morris, Year 4, St Andrew's Methodist Primary School, Farnworth and Worsley Circuit

Times and seasons (Derek Jackson)

Bring me back to you, Lord.
Each day I start afresh,
but there are so many distractions.
Bring me back to you, Lord.
Quieten me, still me.
Help me to be in your presence.
Bring me back to you, Lord. Amen.

Victoria Middleton,
Gnosall Chapel, Stafford Circuit

Lord of heaven and earth, times and seasons, and all people in every place,
we thank you for the rhythms that have their origins in you:
the rhythm of our days, weeks, months and years;
the rhythm of our winter, spring, summer and autumn;
the rhythm of birth, growth, decay and death;
and the rhythm of church life, home life, work life, and relaxation.
You have commanded us
to be still and know that you are God,
not to become weary in doing good,
and to walk with you in wholehearted devotion and faithfulness.
Help us to nurture, maintain and enjoy the good rhythms, Lord,
and to allow you to redeem those that are out of kilter with your will. Amen.

Sam McGuffin, Lakelands District Superintendent, Methodist Church in Ireland

Thank you, Lord, for this sleepless night, for the chance to bring friends to your throne; for pleasant moments remembering, just lying here quietly alone; for the chance to work out a problem free from the noise of the day; for the silence so thickly around me; for making it easy to pray; for the joy of writing a letter, thinking of friends far away; for my books, for poetry, music, and things crowded out in the day; for these long lonely hours I thank you; for blessings received thankfully, and the greatest blessing, my friend of the night, is that you are here with me. Amen.

Greta Stratford, local preacher, Grantham

Lord of all generations
We pray for our young people,
surrounded by conflicting voices,
and challenging choices;
guide those who teach,
direct and support them
and give them wisdom, Lord.

We pray for those stressed by work
and those unable to find employment;
give them stamina to keep going
and trust in your good purposes.
Guard and guide them, Lord.

We pray for our elderly,
coping with increasing frailty,
adjusting to loss and change,
facing an uncertain future;
comfort them with your presence,
and your unfailing love.

Lord who made us,
and keeps us throughout our lives,
in your unchanging care;
send us, in your strength,
to those who need our help. Amen.

Hilary Creed, Trinity Bromley URC

We pray for our young people
(© Anya Goldsack, used with permission)

That was then.
Now is now.
That was seeking.
Now is waiting?
No, not waiting.
More ... abiding.

Geraldine Pedroza

Creator God, when our loved ones begin to forget, we ask you keep them mindful of you.
When our loved ones begin to wander, we ask you to keep them safe.
When dementia makes their bodies frail, we ask you to keep them strong.
For the carers, always in demand, we ask for your guiding hands.
As family mourn a person not yet dead, but who seems gone,
we ask for your comfort and care.
When the time to say a final goodbye comes,
we ask for faith strong enough to know our loved ones have walked that sacred walk
and now reside with you in their heavenly home. Amen.

Sally Cooper, community development worker, Farnworth and Worsley Circuit

DAY 1

Praying with all creation

Keep us safe in your arms, O Lord, that we may have nothing to fear. Let us rely on you in all things that nothing may impede our salvation. Let us love and serve you always, that at your bidding we may enter the presence of your glory; through Christ our Lord. Amen.

John Henry Newman (1801-1890)

Thank you for another day (Graham Thompson)

The incredible gift
Thank you for another day.
Crisp air of a new beginning.
Red sun rising.
Fields of white fog.
Fox cubs lolling by the railway
line. All fresh and freely given.
No one has seen this day before.
Thank you. Amen.

Fiona Marshall, writer, London

We give thanks for the commitment of climate-change advocates, in whatever guise, who boldly challenge the status quo, and give a voice to the voiceless all around the world who are actually suffering the effects of climate change right now.
We pray for politicians and negotiators, that they will make ethical and just decisions, based on science, and not political interests;
for the voiceless and the people who suffer most and contribute least to climate change;
for climate justice and fairness, that everyone may be able to have a dignified existence;
that we will open our ears to hear the cries of the suffering and acknowledge that climate change is a problem for everyone. Amen.

Julia Edwards, mission partner, Fiji

Gracious, liberating God, we enjoy so many freedoms in this culture in which we live.
We pray your forgiveness for the freedoms which we abuse, as we squander the precious resources of this planet, this earth which you have created and placed into our care as your stewards, your caretakers.
Forgive us for our carelessness.
Help us today to value life in all its forms, to treasure and nurture and protect the gifts which you have entrusted to us.
We pray in the name of Christ. Amen.

Anne Browse, President, Methodist Women in Britain, 2015-2017

Freedom is indivisible; the chains on any one of my people were the chains on all of them, the chains on all of my people were the chains on me. Nelson Mandela

Loving God, remind us to pause
when our freedoms come in the form of another's chains:
our freedom to shop when we choose
means another cannot spend time with family;
our freedom to buy inexpensive clothes
means another cannot earn enough to eat;
our freedom to use cheap fuel
means another suffers the consequences of climate change.

Freedom is indivisible.
Unless all are free, we all are diminished,
because you created each one of us in your image.

Liberating God,
we know that sharing your freedoms may come at a cost.
Help us to bear that cost joyfully,
in the knowledge that we are doing your will. Amen.

Rachel Lampard,
Vice-President, British Methodist Conference, 2016/2017

God of compassion,
free me from what is holding me back.
Help me let go of the hurts I cling to.

In my freedom, give me direction,
in my sharing, give me courage,
in my journeying, give me hope.

And through it all, may your kingdom come. Amen.

Paul Wood,
Ministry Development Coordinator, Connexional Team

In a world where we can 'tweet', 'pin', 'like' and 'share'
on social media without thought of punishment,
bring to our hearts and minds, God of wisdom,
those who do not have the freedoms we have
and help us to use our freedom
as a positive influence on those we share with. Amen.

Tim Annan, Methodist Youth President, 2016/2017

President of the British Methodist Conference
Roger Walton

Vice-President
Rachel Lampard

Youth President
Tim Annan

Officers of the Conference

Secretary of the Conference
Gareth Powell

Assistant Secretary of the Conference
Helen Cameron

Conference Officer for Legal and Constitutional Practice
Louise Wilkins

The Methodist Diaconal Order

Warden
Karen McBride

Deputy Warden
Richard Goldstraw

British Connexional Team

Connexional Secretary
Doug Swanney

Cluster Heads
Martin Ashford
Jude Levermore
Nick Moore

DAY 2

Praying with Christians in West Africa

The Gambia

Methodist Bishop
Hannah Faal-Heim

Sierra Leone

Methodist President
Albert Beah

Lord, forgive our sins both past and present; forgive the wrong-doing we have sought to conceal from others and attempted to hide from ourselves; forgive our trespasses against your goodness and love; and heal us with your pardon, through the merits of your Son, our Saviour Jesus Christ. Amen.

John Donne (1572-1631)

We pray for the peoples of **West Africa** as they emerge from the horror of the Ebola crisis. As normality is restored, we remember with gratitude those selfless healthcare professionals who risked, and sometimes gave, their own lives to care for others. We hold before you those families and communities that still suffer because the magnitude of their loss is so great. Comfort the bereaved and the grieving; grant them consolation. As the lights of the world's media are dimmed may the light of your love shine brightly. Let those who still need our help know that they are not forgotten. Grant them hope for the future, we pray. Amen.

Wendy Kilworth-Mason,
superintendent minister, Whitehaven Circuit

Ever-flowing God, meandering gently through our lives and leading us beside still waters, we pray for those whose lives draw sustenance from **the Gambia** River. As the darker salt water from the sea and the lighter fresh water from the river come together and flow side by side, may all people share harmony and freedom, working alongside each other for the growth of your kingdom. Amen.

Hilary Cheng, minister, Forest Circuit

We give thanks for the diversity of the work being undertaken by the Methodist Church throughout the Gambia: tending the sick, teaching the young in the Church, educating from the nurseries through to the Academy, equipping young people in all areas of education and with a knowledge of Christ and his love for all.
We pray for Bishop Hannah Faal-Heim, and all the ministers and leaders of the churches, that they may share the gospel of love.

Margaret Gardner, Birmingham District representative,
MWiB Connexional Forum

Children at the Bethel Nursery School in Banjul enjoying the feeding programme (Margaret Gardner)

Dublin District (Ireland)

Superintendent
Andrew Dougherty

We give thanks for new circuit boundaries that have been graciously established for the sake of mission and outreach;
for the integration of the Dublin Korean Church and its ministry among homeless people, students and the wider Asian community.
We pray for the New Irish who teach others in their community so much about freedom in worship, faith and what it means to be church in the twenty-first century;
for societies which struggle to make painful decisions about their purpose and future;
for ministers who are overworked and struggle to prioritise what is most important in ministry.

London District

Chairs
Nigel Cowgill
Michaela Youngson
(vacancy)

We give thanks for the ministry team of the diaconal order within the London District, who work within a variety of contexts, transforming churches and communities;
for the Whitechapel Mission and The Queen Victoria Seaman's Rest, whose work continues to bring signs of hope to people in the East End of London.
We pray for the continued development of chaplaincy in universities, colleges, schools, hospices, hospitals, prisons, commerce, airports and retail across the District;
for the District Leadership Team as they work with the DMLN in the creation of a Lay Leadership course to enable new leaders to become fruitful and faithful disciples of the gospel.

> God of love, we are called to acts of practical
> love and service, locally, nationally and globally,
> we are called to give a voice to the voiceless
> and to speak out against injustice.
> We are called today to remember homeless people,
> migrants and refugees,
> to weep with compassion as many have done today,
> to ask what we can do and then to do it.
> Help us to show your love
> and hope to all we meet this day. Amen.
>
> *Nigel Cowgill, London District Chair*

Deacon Richard Goldstraw receives a Street Pastor award (Jonny Back)

DAY 3

Praying with Christians in West Africa

Loving God, in whose covenant of grace we are called to love you, not as we ought but as we are able, keep us sincere in our discipleship and faithful to our calling; through the merits of your Son our Saviour, Jesus Christ. Amen.

Thomas Ken (1637-1711)

Benin

Methodist President
Nicodème Alagbada

Scholarship Students
Ezin Anatole Ohouko (in Canada)
Paul Tiburce Kpamegan
Nounagnon Adolphe Zannou-Tchoko
Stéphane Théophile Djekinnouu
Onibon Kingnide Albert (all in Cameroon)

Mission Partners
Michael and Joanna Tettey, Joelle and Janelle (ad/m)

Côte d'Ivoire

Methodist Bishop
Benjamin Boni

Togo

Methodist President
Martine Grace Zinsou-Lawson

We give thanks for the peaceful and harmonious municipal, local and presidential elections in **Benin**;
for all those who are helping to restore Radio Hosanna, The Voice of Hope, which was damaged by a fire in 2015.
We pray that God's mercy may bring an end to global terrorism; for the work of the Church and the spreading of God's word in the North of Benin.

Nicodème Alagbada, President, Église Protestante Méthodiste du Bénin

We pray that the **Côte d'Ivoire** will know a real reconciliation following years of conflict and division in both Church and state. We give thanks for the calmer atmosphere prevailing now, and we pray that the people of the Côte d'Ivoire may accept each others' differences and engage in a peace process, so that political prisoners may be released and exiles may return.
We pray that all will work together towards lasting harmony and security, resting always in close contact with God.

Benjamin Boni, Bishop, United Methodist Church, Côte d'Ivoire

Migrant God, free from borders,
your presence spans the universe.
In all our journeys we find you with us and within us.
In Jesus you reveal yourself taking sanctuary on earth,
in flesh and blood, choosing to pitch a tent among mortals,
with nowhere to lay your head.
We behold you still in the face of those who are uprooted
from their homes by war, poverty and persecution.
We bless you for their courage and resilience
in seeking freedom and sanctuary.
Grant to them safety in all their travail and travels.
Give to all who receive them the capacity to listen
as they share their stories
of a search for justice, freedom and peace. Amen.

Inderjit Bhogal, Learning and Development Officer (Ministry Development), Bristol and West Midlands

We give thanks for the ministry of the HIV Chaplain in Brighton
and for all of the chaplains across the District;
for the District's work in Malta, including the development of a
regular service on Gozo and the ongoing work with refugees;
for the response of Christians in Kent to offer friendship,
support and accommodation to refugees.
We pray for refugees, especially unaccompanied minors;
for those who work in the transport and haulage industry and
for the Border Force and UK Visa and Immigration;
for the churches in Gibraltar and Soto Grande;
for the ecumenical Pioneer Ministry beginning on former army
land in Aldershot.

Liberating God, we praise you for the gift of new life
and the promise that all things will be set free
and will obtain the freedom of the glory of the children of God.
We delight in the joy that comes
from knowing the help of your Spirit in our weakness;
the peace that knowing nothing in all creation
can separate us from your love in Christ Jesus
and the hope that all things will work together
for good for those who love you.
Draw us more fully into your life-giving, loving and liberating
purpose for all creation. Amen.
Based on Romans 8

John Hellyer, South East District Chair

Loving God, as we allow your Spirit to challenge and change us,
may love warm our hearts towards you and others;
may joy smile brightly;
may peace be the foundation upon which we build our actions;
may patience slow us down so we listen in an intolerant world;
may kindness make us generous
to those who see the world differently to us
and goodness be released in acts of that generosity;
may faithfulness steady all our relationships;
may gentleness whisper beauty to those who would hear us;
may self-control limit our excesses.
These things are the expression of your Spirit living and
breathing in us. Amen.

Brian Anderson,
President, Methodist Church in Ireland, 2015/2016

South East District

Chair
John Hellyer

Assistant Chairs
Conrad Hicks
Philip Luscombe
Rose Westwood

Irish Connexional Team

President
William Mullally

Lay Leader of the Conference
Fergus O'Ferrall

Secretary of the Conference
John Stephens

Secretary of MMS (Ireland)
Laurence Graham

Home Mission Secretary
Heather Morris

World Mission and Development Officer
Tim Dunwoody

DAY 4

Praying with Christians in West Africa

Gracious God, let the light of your face shine upon us. Let your peace rule in our hearts, your strength be our song and your grace sufficient for our needs. Prepare us for the events of each day that we may take up our cross and follow in the steps of our Lord and Saviour, Jesus Christ. Amen.

Matthew Henry (1662-1714)

Lord, we give thanks for the relative peace **Ghana** has enjoyed as a country;
for the work and care of the former presiding Bishop, the Most Revd Professor Emmanuel K Asante, and for the invaluable services he has rendered to both the Church and the state;
for the election and induction into office of a new Presiding Bishop, the Most Revd Titus Awotwi Pratt, and the election and induction of six new Bishops and five new Lay Chairmen for the Methodist Church in Ghana.
We pray for the wisdom, strength and the empowerment of the Holy Spirit for the leadership of the Methodist Church in Ghana;
for the vision of the Methodist Church in Ghana to found 300 new churches, and grow the material and spiritual resources of the Church.

Samuel Adu-Boateng, Director, Evangelism, Mission and Renewal Directorate, Methodist Church in Ghana

You came into the world

Lord Jesus, you came into the world to bring peace –
  may we know that peace in our hearts and lives.
You came into the world to bring freedom –
  may all who are trapped in poverty and hunger, and all who are prisoners of conscience know that freedom in their lives.
You come into the world to bring unity –
  may nations, communities and especially churches, be united in spirit, working to one end, the salvation of all.
You came into the world to bring justice –
  may all who have been wronged be vindicated, and all who have been aggressors be brought to repentance.
You came into the world to be love –
  may we all exercise Christlike love and care among others, and know ourselves both loving and loved through him. Amen.

Inspired by Ephesians 2:11-22

Equatorial Guinea

Methodist President
Norberto Dioso Bonde

Ghana

Methodist Presiding Bishop
Titus Awotwi Pratt

Mission Partner
Pat Jamison (n)

Amos Kyere, Methodist minister at Nkoranza Methodist Church, Ghana receives a copy of the Prayer Handbook from Susan Hatton (Jeanette van Galen)

Midlands and Southern District (Ireland)

Superintendent
Denis Maguire

We thank God for outreach initiatives of practical Christianity being offered across the Midlands and Southern District, making faith real in a secular society;
for multi-ethnic congregations, whose diversity and culture bless the District's churches with fresh expressions of worship and growing congregations;
for the staff who cover large geographical areas, and bring their gifts, talents and abilities to the ministry in the District with such enthusiasm and grace.
We pray for Denis Maguire, the new district superintendent, that he may know the blessing of God's leading and be filled with wisdom and grace in the Holy Spirit.

Bedfordshire, Essex and Hertfordshire District

Chair
David Chapman

We give thanks for outreach through foodbanks in the Bedfordshire, Essex and Hertfordshire District;
for probationers and ministers in their early years and the enthusiasm they bring;
for work in schools, for the ministers and lay members who lead assemblies, for Open the Book and Godly Play programmes.
We pray for David Chapman, the new District Chair;
for the new Pioneer Ministry in the Colchester Circuit;
for churches in North Bedfordshire involved in training through the Arthur Rank Germinate initiative.

We remember that, from the time of Abraham, God has called people to travel and change.
We give thanks to all who have responded to that call, and have given us the freedoms that we enjoy today.
We pray for refugees and those who have had to flee their countries of origin, seeking sanctuary, new life and freedom in Britain and other European countries.
As we welcome newcomers, may strangers become friends, and may we be open to the insights new people bring.
Remove the blinkers from our eyes and broaden our vision.
May we remember that we are all one people, the human race. Amen.

Anne Brown, Leeds District Chair,
former Bedfordshire, Essex and Hertfordshire District Chair

DAY 5

Praying with Christians in West Africa

Lord Jesus Christ, draw our hearts to yours with a love that is irresistible; unite our hearts to yours with a love that is inseparable, and bind our hearts to yours with a love that immeasurable; now and for ever. Amen.

Miles Coverdale (1488-1568)

Nigeria

Methodist Prelate
Kalu Chukwuemeka Uche

Mission Partners
Hans and Mary Van den Corput, Marcel and Maurice (d)

Scholarship Student
Ekeke Innocent (in Ghana)

Cameroon

Moderator of the Presbyterian Church
Fonki Samuel Forba

Scholarship Students
Nyuyki Peter (in South Africa)
Aboseh Ngwana (in Britain)
Nekongo Peter Ekumi (in Germany)

We give thanks for Methodist leadership in **Nigeria**.
We pray for free and fair elections in Nigeria;
for the work of the Ozuzuoke Retreat Centre.
for peace and good governance in Africa.

Albert Salvador, administrator, Ozuzuoke Retreat Centre

We give thanks for the one global mission and vision of Methodism and for the freedom to share the gospel, especially through the Nigerian Methodist Chaplaincy, UK/Ireland;
for a smooth democratic transition in Nigeria.
We pray that the Lord in his mercy will raise up more intercessors for the Church and the renewal of its leadership;
for discernment and wisdom for Nigerian leaders as they find the best response to Islamic State, Boko Haram and other jihadist terrorist groups;
for the grace for Nigeria's Christians to stand up for Christ in these terrible times;
that the Church would regain its sense of unified truth.

Deji Okegbile, Nigerian Methodist Chaplaincy, UK/Ireland

Lord, we pray that you will hear our prayer on behalf of your children in the Republic of **Cameroon**.
You are the God of the oppressed and the helpless. Your plan and will for humanity is not founded on discrimination, but on freedom, love, happiness and wholeness, and so we pray for the political leaders of Cameroon, that they may not allow themselves to bring about hardship, pain, anger and frustration on the minority Anglophone community.
Lord, nothing is impossible for you; there is no heart too hard for you to change, there is no hand too big and heavy for you to lift up, there is no army too strong for you to overrun.
We bring the government and peoples of Cameroon before you, that you may bring about your will and an end to discrimination, corruption and terrorism.

Fonki Samuel Forba, Moderator, Presbyterian Church in Cameroon

Birmingham District

Chair
Ian Howarth

We give thanks for work on building community cohesion between faith groups in Birmingham, particularly in Lozells and Saltley;
for the work of Adavu, the District project on trafficking, in partnership with Restore and Citizens UK, which helps refugees and those who have been trafficked;
for new ventures in growing discipleship, particularly the Holy Habits programme across the whole of the Birmingham Circuit, and the growth of Jazz Church.
We pray for the District as it develops its vision to encourage new disciples and for a growth in the depth of discipleship and the transformation of communities;
that the work of the church in Malvern may be the catalyst for a discussion within the community about wider social and political issues.

God of us all, we thank you that you place us in community,
to enable and encourage each other, to share and grow together.
Help those of us who are usually silent or silenced, to speak and be heard.
Help those of us who are always heard,
to learn to make space for others to have voice.
Help us all to be people who listen with our hearts,
value each other's differences, and work together
as we listen to your word and your wisdom.
Please broaden our minds and hearts to be in tune with yours,
that we may see as you see, and love as you love.
Help us to recognise that,
in enabling and encouraging each other with your kindness,
our communities, and each of us in them, may grow and flourish. Amen.

Ruth Yorke, deacon, Birmingham District

When I pray, Lord, I say the lines easily,
but when things get tough, the words are hard to obey.
Enable me Lord, to live the words I pray.
When I feel I want to do the opposite, please strengthen me,
for I know it is these testing times that bring me closer to you.
When I do your will, Lord, the weight is lifted,
peace floods my being
and I am a step closer learning to live in your freedom.
Thank you. Amen.

Victoria Middleton, Gnosall Chapel, Stafford Circuit

DAY 6

The Methodist Church of Southern Africa

Methodist Presiding Bishop
Ziphozihle Siwa

Scholarship Student
Juliet Windvogel
(in Britain)

South Africa

Mission Partners
Stephen° and Jane° Day (m/th)

Botswana

Lesotho

Mozambique

Swaziland

Namibia

Scholarship Students
Kasembele Massamba
Kameya Maina Manyonga
(both in South Africa)

Praying with Christians in Southern Africa

God, beyond all our naming, the glory of creation reaches out to you. God, beyond all our reasoning, the voice of the universe sounds your praise; God, beyond all our knowing, all that live find their destiny in your presence. Amen.

Gregory of Nazianzus (329-389)

We thank God for the rich diversity of languages, cultures and traditions in **South Africa**. We rejoice when, in the midst of incredible diversity, people discover and value their unity in Christ. We celebrate 40 years since the ordination of the first women ministers by the Methodist Church of Southern Africa.
We pray for courage for the Churches in South Africa to embrace vulnerability and seek unity in diversity, trust in place of suspicion, peace in place of fear;
for Magnify, a programme designed to develop women leaders within the Church in South Africa;
for communities living with the effects of drought.

Stephen Day, mission partner,
The Methodist Church of Southern Africa

We pray for the people and Churches of **Botswana** and for our fellow Methodists scattered over that huge country;
for the natural resources of Botswana, such as its diamonds, which have enabled economic development.
Yet Botswana, as with so much of Southern Africa, is repeatedly afflicted by drought, which brings suffering and poverty to rural dwellers and increasing problems of water supply for urban dwellers. In the good times and in the difficult times we pray that Christ may guide the leaders and people of Botswana. Amen.

Jennifer Potter, minister, Wesley's Chapel, London

We give thanks that a Methodist manse has been built by church members near Chimoio in **Mozambique** with money given by the Methodist Church in Britain;
for the initiative to establish a Boys' Brigade in Mozambique;
for the extraordinary natural resources within Mozambique.
We pray for peace and constructive dialogue between Mozambicans of differing political persuasions;
for the Igreja Metodista Wesleyana and other Methodist Churches.

Malcolm Oliver, former mission partner, Mozambique

Bolton and Rochdale District

Chair
Paul Martin

We give thanks for the new buildings across the Bolton and Rochdale District which are signs of hope.
We are heartened by the desire and commitment among the people of the District to make these buildings serve communities and demonstrate God's love.
We celebrate the degree of support and mutual co-operation across circuit boundaries within the District.
We are grateful for the opportunities for mission and evangelism in the Methodist and Methodist/Anglican Schools, and the engagement with community primary schools.
We pray for the developing relationships in the North West and Mann region, asking for God's wisdom in decisions about which structures will best promote the kingdom.
We pray that God will guide circuits and local churches to make best use of their resources, especially in areas of deprivation.
We ask for an outpouring of God's spirit on the District, so that the people there may increasingly know the love of Jesus and make the love of Jesus known.

Liberating God, your Son, Jesus Christ came
so that we might have life in all its fullness.
In your love for us, give us the insistence of Legion,
so that we might be freed from turmoil to find peace.
Give us the curiosity of the woman at the well,
so that we might be freed from ignorance to find knowledge.
Give us the responsiveness of Zacchaeus,
so that we might be freed from greed to find generosity.
Give us the persistence of the widow before the judge,
so that we might be freed from injustice to find justice.
Give us the determination of Peter,
so that we might be freed from dithering to find decisiveness,
Give us the boldness of the woman of Nain,
so that we might be freed from timidity to find proclamation.
Give us the honesty of Thomas,
so that we might be freed from doubt to find faith.
Give us the courage of the women at the tomb,
so that we might be freed from sadness to find joy.
Give us your Spirit,
so that we might be freed from darkness to find light. Amen.

Paul Martin, Bolton and Rochdale District Chair

Freed from turmoil to find peace (Paul Martin)

DAY 7

Praying with Christians in Southern Africa

Be to us, O Lord Jesus Christ, the table set for all, the light radiating from your saints, the sun shining in our midst, and the joy prepared for your people; now and for ever. Amen.

Symeon the New Theologian (949-1022)

Zimbabwe

Methodist Presiding Bishop
Solomon Zwana

Mission Partners
Jonathan and Isobel Hill, Stephen and Susanna (ed/sd)

Scholarship Students
Grenwell Chigova
Rachel Makwara
Peter Masvotore
Martin Mujinga
Grecious Mupazviribwo
Joseph Muwanzi
Vincent F Ncube (all in South Africa)
Farai Ngwaru (in Tanzania)

The United Church of Zambia

Synod Bishop
Sydney Sichilima

General Secretary
Peggy Mulambya Kabonde

Mission Partners
Jenny Featherstone (sd) [+CofS]
Keith and Ida Waddell, Mubita and Catriona (ed/m) [+CofS]

Scholarship Students
Sylvia Mukuka (in South Africa)
Christopher Njovu (in Britain)

We give thanks to God for the humility of the people of **Zimbabwe** as they live in hope of a better future while silently struggling with rapid economic decline;
for the growth of Christianity amid an acute shortage of basic necessities, crippling unemployment, greed, corruption and declining life expectancy following the collapse of the health sector.
We pray for improved governance and better distribution of Zimbabwe's plentiful natural resources;
for voices for the voiceless, dignity for the dying, food for the hungry, jobs for the seeking, shelter for the homeless;
for better social security, fairness in policing and for peace, prosperity and justice for all citizens.

Freddy Takavarasha, Zimbabwean minister working in Norwich

We give thanks for the hard work of the teaching staff at the United Church of **Zambia** Chodort Training Centre that makes it a centre of excellence;
for the skills of the carpenters which are increasing the good reputation of the centre's workshop in the community.
We pray for a stabilisation in the Zambian economy as prices continue to rise every few months;
for the under-educated youth of Zambia, that they may be given a chance to learn trade skills and so increase their chances of climbing out of poverty;
for the students and carpenters at the United Church of Zambia Chodort Training Centre;
that links between Chodort and the local community and the local and national government may be strengthened.
that it may be possible to start a student accommodation building programme in 2016 to allow young people from rural areas to study at Chodort.

Jenny Featherstone, mission partner, Zambia

Lakelands (Ireland)

Superintendent
Samuel McGuffin

We give thanks for a strong emphasis on prayer and outreach in the churches of the Lakelands District;
for faithful work by ministers, stewards and leaders across the District;
for the financial and prayer support of the wider Connexion.
We pray for a clearer vision of what is possible and what is necessary;
for a stronger commitment to what is clear and plain;
for a greater willingness to follow through on commitment.

Bristol District

Chair
Jonathan Pye

We give thanks for all those involved in the work of Methodist Schools in the Bristol District;
for all who work with the elderly and frail and for the residential and home care supported by the Church in the District.
We pray for all those, lay and ordained, who are engaged in pastoral work in both rural and urban communities;
for the renewed work of the Bristol Methodist Centre among the vulnerable in its new premises.

You are generous, God,
you open your hands and you fill our lives with your blessings;
you open your heart and you fill our lives with your love.
Teach us to be generous as you are generous;
and free us to share all that we have and are
with our sisters and brothers, whoever they may be.
Make us compassionate in all things,
so that what we do in your name kindles hope in others
and reflects your loving concern for all creation. Amen.

Jonathan Pye, Bristol District Chair

John Wesley (Stephen Wild)

We pray for the Horsefair Project which will provide new facilities for education, hospitality and mission at the New Room, Bristol.
We pray for visitors who come from all over the world and just down the street, who connect with the story of the Wesleys;
for school groups who come to discover more about Methodism and its relevance today.
We pray that the new facilities will contribute to the New Room's commitment to share God's love with those in Bristol and beyond.

Mandy Briggs, Education Officer, The New Room, Bristol

DAY 8

Praying with Christians in East Africa

Jesus, by your wounded feet, direct our path. Jesus, by your nailed hands, move us to deeds of love. Jesus, by your pierced side, purify our desires. Jesus, by your crown of thorns, annihilate our pride. Jesus by your broken heart, knit ours to yours. Amen.

Richard Crashaw (1613-1649)

Kenya (including Tanzania and Uganda)

Methodist Presiding Bishop
Joseph Ntombura Mwaine

Mission Partners
Claire Smithson (d)
Peter Ensor° (th)

Scholarship Students
Mutua Japhet Naftali
Alice Muthoni Mwila (both in Britain)
Peter Mungiria Mbui (in South Korea)

Rwanda

Methodist Presiding Bishop
Samuel Kayinamura

Scholarship Students
Jeremie Serugo Singaye
Rachel Mukamudenge
Alexandre Ruganzu
Charles Munyamahoro
Seth Bizimana Semabarabara (all in Uganda)
Simeon Mushimiyimana
Casimir Mushimiyimana
Abraham Rugenerwa Ndaye (all in Kenya)

Lord, we give thanks for the growth of the Methodist Church in **Kenya**;
for the liveliness of its worship;
for its concern for mission and evangelism.
We pray that you may continue to give vision and direction to its leaders, provide the resources for its outreach and empower its members to live out their faith in their daily lives.

Peter Ensor, mission partner, Kenya

We give thanks for the continuing witness and ministry of healing of the Maua Methodist Hospital and remember those within it who are facing despair and suffering.
We give thanks for the Presiding Bishop as he leads bishops, ministers and laity through difficult situations.
We pray for compassion for those in need as the hospital serves in the name of Jesus;
for those who are living in fear of the terrorist threat of Al-Shabaab, and for those who are fighting this threat in Kenya.

Barbara Dickinson, former mission partner, Kenya

We give thanks for God's grace which upholds the Church in this risky and challenging world;
for enabling the Methodist Church in **Uganda** to become a synod in its own right;
for the Church's ministry to those in need, especially through the child development centre in Mpumudde village, Jinja District.
We pray for God's guidance and wisdom for the Church leaders that they will give wise leadership to the Church in this transition period;
that God will enable the Church to fulfil its mission of reaching out in word and deed.

Betty Nairuba, Operations Manager, Methodist Church in Uganda

Yr Eglwys Fethodistaidd yng Nghymru

The Methodist Church in Wales

Y Cyngor (The Council)

Synod Cymru Chair
Jennifer Hurd

Wales Synod Chair
Stephen Wigley

We give thanks for ministers from the wider Connexion who come to share in service in Synod Cymru, freely committing themselves to learning a new language in a different culture; for the Wales Synod Enabler Irfan John, the Trinity Centre and others working alongside the City of Sanctuary movement to provide a welcome to asylum seekers and refugees.
We pray that through the translation into Welsh of *Worship: Leading and Preaching*, God will call more Welsh speakers to share freely of themselves by training as worship leaders and local preachers;
that the Holy Spirit will inspire freedom to share the love of Christ for all in acts of service;
that the discipline of learning will bring new freedoms to share for all who are training for ministry in its different forms, and for the DMLN staff as they support and enable this.

God of lightness and life,
in the soaring, swooping and somersaulting of the red kite,
I see the freedom you long to see in your people.
Help us to trust in the thermals and currents of your love,
so that, upheld by you, we may share the joy and liberty
that comes from you alone. Amen.

Dduw goleuni a bywyd,
yn esgyniad, disgyniad a trosben y Barcud Coch,
gwelaf y rhyddid rwyt yn dyheu am ei weld yn dy bobl.
Helpa ni i ymddiried yn haenau ac awelon dy gariad,
er mwyn i ni, wedi ein cynnal gennyt,
rannu'r llawenydd a'r rhyddid
a ddaw oddi wrthyt ti yn unig. Amen.

Jennifer Hurd, Synod Cymru Chair

The soaring of the red kite (Peter Harris)

Lord our God,
your word teaches us that, in showing hospitality to strangers,
we may be welcoming angels into our midst;
help us to make our churches and homes
such places of welcome and sharing
that we may discover anew
the life of your kingdom. Amen.

Stephen Wigley, Wales Synod Chair

DAY 9

Praying with Christians in Latin America

Brazil

Methodist Bishop
Adonias Pereira

Scholarship Students
Group Training:
Women in the Ways of Mission (in Brazil)
Group Training:
Wesleyan Theology (in Latin America Caribbean)

Argentina

Methodist Bishop
Frank de Nully Brown

Colombia

Head of Church
Juan Alberto Cardona

Scholarship Students
Hugo Oquendo Torres
Group Training:
Intensive Pastoral Training Course (both in Colombia)

Venezuela

Methodist President
Francisco Mendoza Bracho

Lord, we bring to you a priceless treasure, greater than the mountains, wider than the world, and deeper than the ocean. We offer you the greatest of all gifts, higher than the heavens, more glorious than the sun and weightier than the whole earth; even the offering of our own heart, to be yours now and for ever. Amen.

Mechtild of Magdeburg (c. 1210-1280)

We pray for the people of **Brazil** as they suffer the effects and after effects of the Zika epidemic which has been strongly linked with a spike in cases of microcephaly;
for babies who are born with this condition, and for their parents and carers;
for scientists, doctors and governing authorities who are trying to find a way of preventing the spread of the virus.

Information supplied by the World Church Relationships Office

We thank God for the Methodist Church in **Argentina** which in 2017 celebrates 180 years of Christian testimony;
for the pastoral corps throughout Argentina;
for all the people in Argentina's Christian communities who share the glad salvation tidings.
We pray for the families who have been affected by floods in Concordia and Colón, where Methodist communities have sheltered people;
for all that comes after an environmental catastrophe and will continue in the coming months.

Frank de Nully Brown, Bishop,
Argentine Evangelical Methodist Church

Blessed are the peacemakers, for they will be called children of God. (Matthew 5:9)

We praise you, our creator, for the dialogue of the peace process in **Colombia** after more than 50 years of war and conflict. We give you thanks because soon Colombia will finally fulfil its dream of lasting peace. We ask for your continuing protection and guidance in this peace process, that your mighty hand will be upon every decision and dialogue, and that you will strengthen each party in the discussion* as well as the Colombian people, that they will not fail in their commitment to peace-building.

Amparo Beltrán Acosta,
Co-director of CEPALC, the Latin America Media Centre

**the government and the guerrilla groups*

Cumbria District

Chair
Richard Teal

Ullswater
(Joan and Ray Wager)

We give thanks for the remarkable 'Spirit of Cumbria' which brought so many people together in the effort to rebuild their lives and businesses after the 2015 floods;
for the ecumenical relief work which has built bridges of mutual respect, and has been a witness to a united Church.
We pray for the communities within the District: may they quickly recover, not only physically, but also in mind and spirit and may they feel strengthened by your presence;
for the development of Mission Communities: may your love shine through their actions and may they be beacons of hope and signs of your grace;
for mission projects within the District: may they be fresh expressions of discipleship and faith.

Gracious God, you are the same yesterday, today and forever. We celebrate this amazing truth about your nature and deeply trust it in our hearts. Yet there are occasions and times in our lives when we acknowledge that faith feels very different, when life is hard, dark or bleak and the way ahead seems unclear. In those times, loving God, focus our minds and hearts on those moments and times when your grace has surprised us and faith has been renewed, hope has come alive and love has been reborn.
O God, you are the same yesterday, today and forever and so we praise you. Amen.

Mel Beavan, deacon, North Cumbria Circuit

Enable me, O God, to collect and compose my thoughts before an immediate approach to you in prayer. May I be careful to have my mind in order when I take upon myself the honour to speak to the Sovereign Lord of the universe, remembering that upon the temper of my soul depends, in very great measure, my success. You are infinitely too great to be trifled with, too wise to be imposed on by a mock devotion, and abhor a sacrifice without a heart. Help me to entertain an habitual sense of your perfections, as an admirable help against cold and formal performances. Save me from engaging in rash and precipitate prayers and from abrupt breaking away to follow business or pleasure as though I had never prayed. Amen.

Susanna Wesley (1669-1742)

DAY 10

Praying with Christians in Latin America

Uruguay

Methodist President
Alfredo Alcarraz

Bolivia

Methodist Bishop
Modesto Mamani

Scholarship students
Group Training:
Specialisation in School Chaplaincy (in Bolivia)

Chile

Methodist Bishop
Pedro Correa Montecinos

Peru

Methodist Bishop
Samuel Aguilar Curi

Scholarship Students
Group Training:
Biblical, Theological and Pastoral Training (in Peru)

Ecuador

Methodist Bishop
Silvio Cevallos

O Holy Spirit, giver of life and light, breath of all creatures, purifier of all souls and healer of all wounds; be fire to our heart, light to our path and friend for our journey; and this for your own love's sake. Amen.

Hildegard of Bingen (1098-1179)

We give thanks for the multilingual and multicultural ministry of the Methodist Church in **Bolivia**;
for the growth of its work in the local churches and the national leadership of the Methodist Church in Bolivia.
We pray for peace and justice in Bolivia and around the world;
for Bolivia's economic development;
for wisdom for the leaders of the Methodist Church in Bolivia.

Javier Rojas Teran, late Bishop,
Evangelical Methodist Church of Bolivia (d.2016)

Good God and Celestial Father, we ask for help to share our lives with others, with those who are not the same as us. Free us from pride and indifference. Help us especially to give an important part of our lives to those who are abandoned by society, by their families and by the economic system, and who are adrift and without hope. Help us, Lord, to be aware of them and to offer more of ourselves. Amen.

Pedro Correa Montecinos,
Bishop, Methodist Church in Chile

We give thanks to God for sharing with us the spirit of freedom, charity, compassion and mercy toward our neighbours;
for giving us freedom to share the values of the kingdom of God, justice, peace and love where there is conflict between nations;
for the hope God gives to the people of **Peru** to face challenges.
We pray for comfort and healing for those who grieve for loved ones lost in the violence and social insecurity of Peru;
for elderly people who feel abandoned by their children;
for families who leave their land, houses, and people in search of refuge or a better life;
for the Methodist Church in Peru, that it may fulfil its mission to be light and salt in the life of the nation.

Samuel Aguilar Curi, Bishop, Methodist Church of Peru

North West District (Ireland)

Superintendent
Peter Murray

We give thanks that in each of the six circuits of the North West Ireland District where good work is being done in the name of Jesus, good relations continue to be forged with other Christian communities and barriers continue to be broken down.
We pray for God's help with new ventures in the District;
for Jono and Beth Griffin, who head up the Surf Project in its new base in Portrush;
for the congregation in Limavady where new outreach is taking place under the leadership of Paul Gallucci, and for circuits who received new ministers in July 2016.

Channel Islands District

Chair
David Hinchliffe

We give thanks that the building of the Sark Sanctuary Centre is underway;
for the Guernsey Youth Housing Project run by Action for Children, and their work to support vulnerable young people.
We pray for the MHA care homes, Maison La Corderie and Stuart Court in Jersey and Maison L'Aumone and Maison de Quetteville in Guernsey;
for the community workers of St Helier Methodist Centre and Georgetown Methodist Church in Jersey, who support families in crisis;
for the ecumenical Guernsey Welfare Service, and Philippi Guernsey Counselling Service, an interdenominational Christian charity which offers professional counselling to those of all faiths and none in Guernsey.

God of grace and mercy,
we acknowledge before you that which is so easily hidden,
and the struggles with those things which can imprison and bind us:
struggling to make ends meet;
the challenge of finding affordable housing;
substance abuse;
the stress of finding a place in society again;
damaged and broken relationships;
mental and physical illness.
May we find sanctuary beneath your everlasting arms.
May we offer the love of Christ which sets us free,
and enables us to become the people you call us to be.
In Jesus' name. Amen.

David Hinchliffe, Channel Islands District Chair

Memorial to the safe rescue of passengers from the stricken vessel, *Saint-Malo* at Corbière, Jersey (© David Hinchliffe, used with permission)

DAY 11

Praying with Christians in the Caribbean and the Americas

Let us prefer your presence, O God, to all other company. Let us exalt your name, O Lord, above all other names and let us love your will, O God, beyond all other desires; for the sake of Jesus Christ. Amen.

Therese of Lisieux (1873-1897)

Methodist Church in the Caribbean and the Americas (MCCA)

Connexional Bishop
Otto Wade

Leeward Islands District (MCCA)

District Bishop
Charles Seaton

Guyana District (MCCA)

District Bishop
Glenna Spencer

Panama/Costa Rica District (MCCA)

District Bishop
Heinsley Johnson

Belize/Honduras District (MCCA)

District Bishop
Roosevelt Papouloute

We pray for Bishop Papouloute and all who minister in the **Belize/Honduras** District. We pray that all citizens of Belize and Honduras will be able to experience freedom from poverty, from fear, from violence and from corruption. We praise you for the love and dedication of those working to bring about a transformation in those lands, and pray that your true freedom may be known and experienced by all.

Jamie Williams, United Methodist mission partner, Belize (MCCA) and Maggie Patchett, former mission partner, Belize/Honduras District (MCCA)

We pray for the leaders in government, industry and the Churches of **Guyana**. We pray that those appointed will lead with justice, compassion, humility and equity and use their positions of trust to bring lasting change to the land and its people. We pray that the people of Guyana will work together to bring about freedom from poverty, oppression and hopelessness. May God's people live in unity so that the light and love of Jesus will fill the land, illuminating the darkness and bringing freedom to all.

Carolyn Lawrence, local preacher, Plymouth and Exeter District, former mission partner, Guyana District (MCCA)

We give thanks for the ministry of the Revd Cidaël Calixte, the first presbyter from the Haiti District to work in the **Panama/ Costa Rica** District;
for the growth of the Methodist school in Colon;
for the work of the Revd Juan Simpson who returns to the Panama Circuit after many years of ministry elsewhere.
We pray for the ongoing construction of a church hall for the Isla Colón congregation in the Bocas del Toro Circuit;
for missionary work in the community of Barranco Adentro in the Bocas del Toro Circuit;
for a new boat and presbyter in the Valiente Methodist Mission.

Heinsley Johnson, Bishop, Panama/Costa Rica District (MCCA)

Chester and Stoke-on-Trent District

Chair
Peter Barber

We give thanks for fragile lives that encounter kindness and generosity of spirit in the cafés and coffee bars established by churches across the Chester and Stoke-on-Trent District;
for the night shelters in churches in Stoke, Crewe and Chester as well as the day centres and pop-in facilities provided by increasing numbers of churches;
for the district mission and ministry teams sharing in circuits where there are ministerial vacancies.
We pray for new churches emerging within the District through church-planting, reseeding, pioneering and holy risk taking, that these sparks of the Spirit may become kingdom flames;
for the fulfilment of the need for emerging leadership within churches, circuits and the District.

Fan us with your love (Peter Barber)

Loving God, each day you place before me life and death.
Because you have chosen me, I am free to choose you.
Because you loved me first, I am free to choose to love you.
Because you gave your Son who chose to die for my sins,
I am free to choose to live his life;
life in service faithfully employed.
Today, I choose life in loving and serving you. Amen.

John Bolton, National Advocate, LWPT 2015/2016

Gracious God, known and encountered in broken bread,
grant us the openness to see you in our broken humanity,
the courage to share that common humanity
and the contentment to find in you all we need.

Gracious God, who knew and experienced flight from terror,
grant us the compassion to see and hear you in the faces and cries of refugees,
the willingness to be their voice and to plead their cause,
and the strength to work for justice and peace from sunrise to sunset.

Gracious God, provider of this good and bountiful world,
grant us the wisdom to see it as yours and not ours,
the faith to share it with a generosity of spirit
and the humility of heart to acknowledge it as your good gift to all.

Gracious God, grant us compassion, melt our cold hearts,
give us tears of empathy and sorrow, fan within us your love
so that we may experience the freedom to share your passion,
in your ways, to your praise and glory. Amen.

Peter Barber, Chester and Stoke-on-Trent District Chair

DAY 12

Praying with Christians in the Caribbean and the Americas

South Caribbean District (MCCA)

District Bishop
Cuthbert Edwards

Scholarship Student
Emasseau Pierre (in USA and Jamaica)

Bahamas/Turks and Caicos Islands District (MCCA)

District Bishop
Derek Browne

Dominican Republic

Head of Church
Miguel Angel Cancú

Nicaragua

Head of Church
Eduardo Rodriguez

Mission Partners
Paul Collins and Maura Cook, Scout, Assisi and Saffi (ed)

Grant to us, Lord, purity of heart and strength of purpose; that no passion may hinder us from knowing your will and no weakness from doing it; that in your light we may see light clearly, and in your service find perfect freedom; through Christ our Lord. Amen.

Augustine of Hippo (354-430)

We give thanks for the beauty of the **Bahamas** and the **Turks and Caicos Islands**;
for the jobs that are provided by the tourism industry;
for the freedom to share and express faith in a place where being a member of the Church is seen as the norm;
for the continued work to improve the lives of those living with HIV/AIDS, particularly among the young people of the islands.
We continue to pray for the victims of crime and violence, particularly where gangs are involved;
for those made poorer by the deregulation of gambling houses;
for the future of St Paul's Methodist College, Grand Bahama, where student numbers have decreased and the buildings are in need of repair and renovation.

Eddie Sykes, former mission partner, Bahamas/Turks and Caicos Islands District (MCCA)

We give thanks for the dynamic people of the **South Caribbean**;
for the work of Methcare in Grenada, training young people in practical skills for family life and to gain employment;
for the much-needed health fairs run by the youth of the Methodist Church.
We pray for the staff and students of Wesley College, the only Methodist secondary school in the South Caribbean;
for leaders in Church and government to have vision and courage as they respond to rapidly changing island life, no longer isolated in a hyper-connected world.

Andrew Dye, former mission partner, Grenada

We give thanks for the work of Jackie Emmasseau (NMA) who is supporting local women by teaching them sewing skills that will help their families and boost their confidence.
We pray for women in the Grenada Circuit in the South Caribbean District, MCCA who find themselves the sole breadwinners for their families as well as the main carers of their children.

Information supplied by the World Church Relationships Office

Cornwall District

Chair
Steven Wild

Pattern on a Cornish font (Steven Wild)

We give thanks for the rich heritage of Cornish Methodism
and for centres of phenomenal church growth;
for the Bridge Project on an industrial estate in Launceston,
which connects with the community through a skateboard
park, soft-play area, café and rooms for prayer and counselling;
for street pastors in Truro and other towns, foodbanks, prayer
walking in the Tamar Valley, the Christianity Explored course in
the Liskeard Circuit and The Well at Truro, which offers learning
and leisure activities in the city centre.
We pray for the church centre being built on a new estate in
Newquay, that it may become a place of love and welcome;
for village chapels facing up to change and connecting with
scattered farms and homesteads in new ways;
for the whole people of Cornwall, one of the poorest counties in
Britain, where most jobs are seasonal and unemployment rates
in winter are high.

Eternal God, strong to save,
into this broken world we pray for the blessing of your peace.
Amid its wars and the suffering of the innocent, we pray for your justice.
Be alongside those who serve in our nation's armed forces,
through the rigours of hard training;
in the separation and loneliness of deployment;
facing danger on the front line;
in the uncertainties of service life.
Be with the families that sacrifice their normality to support them.
And where they feed the hungry, console the refugee, confront the pirate,
challenge the smuggler or face the foe,
may they ever remember your calling to follow and serve with love.
Eternal God, may there ever rise to thee,
glad hymns of praise from land, sea and air. Amen.

Mark Noakes, CSFC Chaplain, HMS Raleigh, Cornwall

Loving God,
from his ministry in small towns, villages and hamlets,
your Son calls us to work with him
to create a new community where the values of hospitality,
forgiveness, generosity and mutual care
come before the acquisition of material things.
So may our seemingly insignificant communities
become centres of your transforming love. Amen.

Maureen Edwards, former editor, Methodist Prayer Handbook

DAY 13

Praying with Christians in the Caribbean and the Americas

When the darkness of this world is past, may Christ the Morning Star, bring to all God's saints the promise of the light of life that opens into everlasting day. Amen.

The Venerable Bede (c. 673-735)

Jamaica District (MCCA)

District Bishop
Everald Galbraith

Scholarship Student
Janis Jack-Watson (in Jamaica)

Haiti District (MCCA)

District Bishop
Gesner Paul

Scholarship Student
Chrisnel Lelievre (in Britain)

Mission Partners
John and Sharon Harbottle (d/ed)

Scholarship Students
Group Training:
Formation as Stewards and Worship Leaders (in Haiti)

Cuba
Methodist Bishop
Ricardo Pereira Díaz

Scholarship Students
Group Training:
PhD in Ministry
Enoel Gutiérrez Echevarría
Alfredo R. González Carballosa
Rigoberto Figueroa Yero
Madelaine Cruz Rodríguez
(all in Cuba)

We give thanks for a hurricane-free 2015 in **Jamaica**, even though the drought was severe and resulted in many bush fires; for the very positive trends in Jamaica's economy.
We pray for more candidates for the diaconate and the itinerant presbyterate;
for God's blessings on the income-generating projects as the Church seeks to use what is in its hands for the financial sustainability of the District;
for a return to basic principles of honesty, purity, respect, industriousness and kindness.

Everald Galbraith, Bishop, Jamaica District (MCCA)

Gracious God, we thank you for the 200th anniversary of the Methodist Church in **Haiti** in February 2017;
for the contributions made by the Methodist Church in Haiti over the last two centuries in the fields of evangelism, education, literacy, health and community development;
for lives changed in Haiti, for souls delivered from sin,
for health restored and progress made.
We pray for guidance, love, faith, courage and protection for Christians as they bear witness to and do the work of your kingdom in a country suffering from a socio-political and economic crisis;
for the ministers, lay preachers, evangelists, stewards and social workers as they fulfil their calling to the glory of God.

Marco Depestre Jr, Secretary, Haiti District (MCCA)

Come, Lord Jesus, into the midst of our violence and fear,
to remind us again of the depth of God's love
and free us to be part of your transforming reign. Amen.

Malcolm Atherton, supernumerary minister, Cheshire South Circuit

North East District (Ireland)

Superintendent
William Davison

We give thanks for outreach into local communities in the North East Ireland District;
for growing fellowships of learning and prayer;
for grants which enable societies to carry out refurbishments of halls;
for the establishment of new services for those with dementia and for their families.
We pray for guidance and direction as plans are made for future staffing in the District;
for all leaders and office-bearers, that they may know how much they are valued;
for wisdom in using all the resources provided by members of societies across the District.

Darlington District

Chair
Ruth Gee

We give thanks for the faithful witness of Christians in the rural areas of the Darlington District where resources can be scarce and where loneliness and isolation threaten;
for the Faith and Arts Network events in the Durham and Deerness Valley Circuit which enable expressions of faith through dance, music, photography and other creative arts;
for those responding to a call to ministry in the North East.
We pray for those in our communities who welcome and support the hungry, the homeless and refugees;
for those who have set up and run foodbanks to alleviate hunger in our towns and villages;
for a renewed heart for mission, and a desire to speak about Jesus that cannot be contained because it is like a fire burning in the bones.

For freedom Christ has set us free;
for freedom to love and to be loved,
for freedom to grow and discover.
Freedom to learn,
freedom to thrive,
freedom to laugh,
freedom to play.

For freedom Christ has set us free.
We will not submit again to slavery;
to the slavery of prejudice and hatred,
the slavery of hunger and deprivation,
the slavery of privilege,
the slavery of repression,
the slavery of terror,
the slavery of greed,
the slavery of empty ritual.

For freedom Christ has set us free;
we will not submit again to slavery. Amen.

Ruth Gee, Darlington District Chair

DAY 14

Praying with Christians in North and Central America

Lord, let us not give up your cause, nor abandon your work. Let us not give up the fight. Let us persevere, until we see your kingdom come and enter into your glory. Amen.

Francis Asbury (1745-1816)

United Methodist Church (USA)

Ecumenical Officer to the Council of Bishops
Mary Ann Swenson

The United Church of Canada

General Secretary
Nora Sanders

Mexico

Methodist Bishop
Andrés Hernández Miranda

Puerto Rico

Methodist Bishop
Rafael Moreno Rivas

El Salvador

Methodist President
Juan De Dios Peña

Scholarship Students
Central American students' group training

Guatemala

Methodist Bishop
Tomás Riquiac Ixtan

We give thanks for communities of faith in **Canada** that welcome new immigrants and refugees;
for communities of faith that live and promote harmonious relationships between aboriginal and non-aboriginal people.
We pray for healing initiatives between aboriginal and non-aboriginal people;
for continuing efforts in creation care and changes in mining practices and in fossil fuel consumption;
for churches that struggle to connect meaningfully with multiple cultures, including youth and young-adult cultures;
for an effective church response to the growing secularisation of culture and society.

Alydia Smith, Programme Coordinator, Worship, Music and Spirituality, The United Church of Canada

Dear Lord, we pray that you would accompany the thousands of Latin American migrants from **Mexico** who travel to the US border every year. We ask that you would continue to use local Methodist churches and facilities along the border to meet the needs of these vulnerable migrants, many of whom are women and children, many of the children unaccompanied. May they find refuge, provision, protection and spiritual support through Methodists and other Christians, whose ministry it is to accompany them through the love of Christ. Amen.

Sandra Lopez, WCR Partnership Coordinator, Americas and Caribbean

We pray for families in **El Salvador** whose crops have disappeared in the drought;
for thousands of Salvadoran children who set off on the dangerous journey towards the US border.
We pray that El Salvador will become a safe and prosperous place so that families will no longer be broken up by migration, violence, poverty and infidelity.

from information supplied by Paul Collins and Maura Cook, former mission partners, El Salvador, now serving in Nicaragua

Lectionary Readings and Psalms

Lectionary Readings and Psalms

This selection of readings, hymns and psalms has been prepared by Norman Wallwork. Major holy days and special days of prayer and observation have been included.

For a daily reflection and commentary on the readings visit *A Word in Time* www.methodistchurch.org.uk/bible

A guide to daily prayer

Printed below is one possible way of making use of *Singing the Faith* as a daily prayer companion linked with the material provided each day in the Prayer Handbook and in the centre fold of Lectionary Readings and Psalms.

O Lord, open our lips,
and we shall praise your name.

Hymn – from the Lectionary

Psalm – from the Lectionary

Reading – from the Lectionary

Canticle – from *Singing the Faith*

Sunday	796	A Song of Resurrection
	or 799	*Te Deum Laudamus*
Monday	792	*Benedictus* – The Song of Zechariah
Tuesday	798	Great and Wonderful
Wednesday	791	A Song of Creation
Thursday	797	A Song of Christ's Glory
Friday	795	Saviour of the World
Saturday	793	*Magnificat* – The Song of Mary
	or 794	*Nunc Dimittis* – The Song of Simeon

Prayer of the Day – from the top left hand box of the page for the day in the Handbook

Intercession and Reflection – from the appropriate day of the Handbook
or from pages 2-9 of the Handbook

The Lord's Prayer

The Grace

Week beginning 28 August
22nd in Ordinary Time
Healing Faith

Sun	28	Luke 14:1, 7-14	Singing the Faith 362	Psalm 112
Mon	29*	Matthew 14:1-12	Singing the Faith 732	Psalm 11
Tue	30	Matthew 8:5-13	Singing the Faith 661	Psalm 144
Wed	31	Matthew 8:14-22	Singing the Faith 246	Psalm 145:1-7
Thu	1	Matthew 8:23-27	Singing the Faith 241	Psalm 145:8-21
Fri	2	Matthew 8:28 – 9:1	Singing the Faith 654	Psalm 146
Sat	3	Matthew 9:2-8	Singing the Faith 650	Psalm 147

** Beheading of John the Baptist*

Week beginning 4 September
23rd in Ordinary Time
Wisdom and Knowledge

Sun	4	Luke 14:25-33	Singing the Faith 563	Psalm 139
Mon	5	Proverbs 1:1-7	Singing the Faith 515	Psalm 148
Tue	6	Proverbs 3:1-26	Singing the Faith 677	Psalm 149:1-5
Wed	7	Proverbs 6:12-19	Singing the Faith 508	Psalm 150
Thu	8*	Zechariah 2:10-13	Singing the Faith 325	Psalm 127
Fri	9	Proverbs 8:1-11	Singing the Faith 500	Psalm 1
Sat	10	Proverbs 10:1-11	Singing the Faith 507	Psalm 2:1-8

** Nativity of the Virgin Mary*

Week beginning 11 September
24th in Ordinary Time
Goodness and Mercy

Sun	11*	Luke 15:1-10	Singing the Faith 470	Psalm 51
Mon	12	Proverbs 11:1-12	Singing the Faith 501	Psalm 3
Tue	13	Proverbs 12:10-22	Singing the Faith 499	Psalm 4
Wed	14†	Philippians 2:6-11	Singing the Faith 279	Psalm 22
Thu	15	Proverbs 14:31-35	Singing the Faith 693	Psalm 5:1-8
Fri	16	Proverbs 15:18-33	Singing the Faith 491	Psalm 6:1-9
Sat	17	Proverbs 18:5-12	Singing the Faith 366	Psalm 7:1-11

** Education Sunday † Holy Cross Day*

Week beginning 18 September
25th in Ordinary Time
Words of Wisdom

Sun	18	Luke 16:1-13	Singing the Faith 563	Psalm 113
Mon	19	Proverbs 20:1-11	Singing the Faith 493	Psalm 8
Tue	20	Proverbs 22:1-16	Singing the Faith 123	Psalm 9:1-10
Wed	21*	Matthew 9:9-13	Singing the Faith 653	Psalm 119:65-72
Thu	22	Proverbs 24:23-29	Singing the Faith 490	Psalm 10:1-12
Fri	23	Proverbs 25:1-14	Singing the Faith 550	Psalm 11:1-5
Sat	24	Proverbs 25:15-28	Singing the Faith 256	Psalm 12

** Matthew, Apostle and Evangelist*

Week beginning 25 September
26th in Ordinary Time
Inward Beauty

Sun	25	Luke 16:19-31	Singing the Faith 80	Psalm 146
Mon	26	Proverbs 26:12-28	Singing the Faith 81	Psalm 13
Tue	27	Proverbs 27:1-11	Singing the Faith 695	Psalm 15
Wed	28	Proverbs 30:1-9	Singing the Faith 475	Psalm 16
Thu	29*	Revelation 12:7-12	Singing the Faith 637	Psalm 103
Fri	30	Proverbs 31:10-31	Singing the Faith 608	Psalm 17
Sat	1	Ecclesiastes 1:1-11	Singing the Faith 137	Psalm 18:1-16

** Michael and All Angels*

Week beginning 2 October
27th in Ordinary Time
Law and Grace

Sun	2	Luke 17:5-10	Singing the Faith 509	Psalm 37:1-19
Mon	3	Matthew 12:1-8	Singing the Faith 591	Psalm 19
Tue	4	Matthew 12:9-21	Singing the Faith 247	Psalm 20
Wed	5	Matthew 12:22-32	Singing the Faith 253	Psalm 21:1-7
Thu	6	Matthew 12:38-45	Singing the Faith 255	Psalm 22:1-21
Fri	7	Matthew 12:46-50	Singing the Faith 685	Psalm 22:22-31
Sat	8	Matthew 13:1-17	Singing the Faith 671	Psalm 23

Week beginning 9 October
28th in Ordinary Time
Parables of the Kingdom

Sun	9*	Luke 17:11-19	Singing the Faith 653	Psalm 111
Mon	10	Matthew 13:18-23	Singing the Faith 250	Psalm 24
Tue	11	Matthew 13:24-30	Singing the Faith 408	Psalm 25
Wed	12	Matthew 13:31-35	Singing the Faith 123	Psalm 26
Thu	13	Matthew 13:36-43	Singing the Faith 745	Psalm 27
Fri	14	Matthew 13:44-53	Singing the Faith 493	Psalm 29
Sat	15	Matthew 13:54-58	Singing the Faith 526	Psalm 32

*Prisons week * Prisons Sunday*

Week beginning 16 October
29th in Ordinary Time
Doubting and Trusting

Sun	16	Luke 18:1-8	Singing the Faith 529	Psalm 121
Mon	17	Matthew 14:1-12	Singing the Faith 746	Psalm 33
Tue	18*	2 Timothy 4:5-17	Singing the Faith 664	Psalm 145
Wed	19	Matthew 14:13-21	Singing the Faith 324	Psalm 31:1-8
Thu	20	Matthew 14:22-27	Singing the Faith 517	Psalm 31:9-24
Fri	21	Matthew 14:28-33	Singing the Faith 629	Psalm 34:1-10
Sat	22	Matthew 14:34-36	Singing the Faith 355	Psalm 34:11-22

** Luke, Evangelist*

Week beginning 23 October

30th in Ordinary Time

Messiah and Lord

Sun	23	Luke 18:9-14	Singing the Faith 34	Psalm 84
Mon	24	Matthew 15:1-20	Singing the Faith 251	Psalm 35:9-18
Tue	25	Matthew 15:21-31	Singing the Faith 601	Psalm 36
Wed	26	Matthew 15:32-39	Singing the Faith 153	Psalm 37:1-11
Thu	27	Matthew 16:1-12	Singing the Faith 643	Psalm 37:12-29
Fri	28*	John 15:17-27	Singing the Faith 677	Psalm 117
Sat	29	Matthew 16:13-27	Singing the Faith 748	Psalm 37:30-40

*One World Week * Simon and Jude, Apostles*

Week beginning 30 October

31st in Ordinary Time

Grace Abounding

Sun	30*	Luke 6:20-31	Singing the Faith 746	Psalm 149
Mon	31	Matthew 17:1-8	Singing the Faith 261	Psalm 38:1-9
Tue	1+	Matthew 5:1-12	Singing the Faith 744	Psalm 34:1-10, 22
Wed	2	Matthew 17:9-13	Singing the Faith 551	Psalm 38:10-22
Thu	3	Matthew 17:14-27	Singing the Faith 627	Psalm 39
Fri	4	Matthew 18:1-14	Singing the Faith 420	Psalm 40:1-10
Sat	5	Matthew 18:15-35	Singing the Faith 613	Psalm 41

** All Saints' Sunday + All Saints' Day*

Week beginning 6 November

32nd in Ordinary Time

A Community of Grace

Sun	6	Luke 20:27-38	Singing the Faith 348	Psalm 17:1-9
Mon	7	Matthew 19:13-15	Singing the Faith 537	Psalm 42
Tue	8	Matthew 19:16-22	Singing the Faith 432	Psalm 43
Wed	9	Matthew 19:23-26	Singing the Faith 434	Psalm 44:1-8
Thu	10	Matthew 19:27-30	Singing the Faith 582	Psalm 45
Fri	11	Matthew 20:1-16	Singing the Faith 518	Psalm 46
Sat	12	Matthew 20:17-34	Singing the Faith 611	Psalm 47

Week beginning 13 November

33rd in Ordinary Time

Privilege and Obedience

Sun	13*	Luke 21:5-19	Singing the Faith 696	Psalm 98
Mon	14	Deuteronomy 4:1-14	Singing the Faith 463	Psalm 48
Tue	15	Deuteronomy 4:32-40	Singing the Faith 19	Psalm 49
Wed	16	Deuteronomy 6:4-13	Singing the Faith 73	Psalm 50:1-15
Thu	17	Deuteronomy 10:12-22	Singing the Faith 300	Psalm 51
Fri	18	Deuteronomy 26:16-19	Singing the Faith 122	Psalm 52
Sat	19	Deuteronomy 30:15-20	Singing the Faith 600	Psalm 53

** Remembrance Sunday*

Week beginning 20 November
Week before Advent
Faithful in Ministry

Sun	20*†	Luke 23:33-43	Singing the Faith 777	Psalm 46
Mon	21	Deuteronomy 31:1-8	Singing the Faith 736	Psalm 54
Tue	22	Deuteronomy 31:9-13	Singing the Faith 34	Psalm 55:1-8
Wed	23	Deuteronomy 31:23-28	Singing the Faith 488	Psalm 55:16-22
Thu	24	Deuteronomy 31:30 – 32:14	Singing the Faith 97	Psalm 56
Fri	25	Deuteronomy 32:44-52	Singing the Faith 650	Psalm 57
Sat	26	Deuteronomy 34:1-12	Singing the Faith 669	Psalm 61

** Christ the King † Women Against Violence Sunday*

Week beginning 27 November
1st of Advent
Justice and Sacrifice

Sun	27	Matthew 24:36-44	Singing the Faith 780	Psalm 122
Mon	28	Isaiah 1:1-11	Singing the Faith 727	Psalm 62
Tue	29	Isaiah 1:12-20	Singing the Faith 364	Psalm 63:1-8
Wed	30*	John 1:35-42	Singing the Faith 660	Psalm 27
Thu	1†	Isaiah 1:21-28	Singing the Faith 186	Psalm 64
Fri	2	Isaiah 2:1-5	Singing the Faith 169	Psalm 65
Sat	3	Isaiah 4:2-6	Singing the Faith 390	Psalm 66

** Andrew, Apostle † World AIDS Day*

Week beginning 4 December
2nd of Advent
Vision and Promise

Sun	4	Matthew 3:1-12	Singing the Faith 182	Psalm 72:1-7, 18-19
Mon	5	Isaiah 6:1-8	Singing the Faith 31	Psalm 67
Tue	6	Isaiah 7:1-9	Singing the Faith 160	Psalm 68:1-20
Wed	7	Isaiah 7:10-14	Singing the Faith 176	Psalm 68:24-35
Thu	8*	Song of Solomon 2:1-4	Singing the Faith 457	Psalm 45
Fri	9	Isaiah 10:12-23	Singing the Faith 342	Psalm 69:1-21
Sat	10	Isaiah 11:1-10	Singing the Faith 378	Psalm 69:30-36

** Conception of the Blessed Virgin Mary*

Week beginning 11 December
3rd of Advent
Expectancy and Hope

Sun	11	Matthew 11:2-11	Singing the Faith 172	Psalm 146
Mon	12	Isaiah 25:6-10	Singing the Faith 171	Psalm 71:1-11
Tue	13	Isaiah 26:1-6	Singing the Faith 169	Psalm 71:12-16
Wed	14	Isaiah 26:7-9	Singing the Faith 177	Psalm 71:17-24
Thu	15	Isaiah 29:17-24	Singing the Faith 179	Psalm 73:1-14
Fri	16	Isaiah 30:19-26	Singing the Faith 180	Psalm 73:15-28
Sat	17	Isaiah 35:1-10	Singing the Faith 185	Psalm 75:1-7

Week beginning 18 December
4th of Advent and Christmas
The Coming Light

Sun	18	Matthew 1:18-25	Singing the Faith 178	Psalm 80
Mon	19	Luke 1:5-25	Singing the Faith 188	Psalm 76
Tue	20	Luke 1:26-38	Singing the Faith 187	Psalm 24
Wed	21	Luke 1:39-45	Singing the Faith 183	Psalm 25
Thu	22	Luke 1:46-56	Singing the Faith 181	Psalm 10
Fri	23	Luke 1:57-66	Singing the Faith 174	Psalm 110
Sat	24	Luke 1:67-80	Singing the Faith 188	Psalm 13

Week beginning 25 December
1st of Christmas
The Word Incarnate

Sun	25*	Luke 2:1-20	Singing the Faith 195	Psalm 110
Mon	26†	Acts 7:51-60	Singing the Faith 188	Psalm 13
Tue	27∞	John 21:19b-25	Singing the Faith 366	Psalm 117
Wed	28°	Matthew 2:13-18	Singing the Faith 218	Psalm 124
Thu	29	Hebrews 1:1-4	Singing the Faith 272	Psalm 96:1-6
Fri	30	2 Timothy 1:8-10	Singing the Faith 350	Psalm 96:7-10
Sat	31	Philippians 2:6-11	Singing the Faith 251	Psalm 96:11-13

** Christmas Day † Stephen, Martyr ∞ John, Evangelist ° Holy Innocents*

Week beginning 1 January
2nd of Christmas
Glory Revealed

Sun	1*	John 1:1-18	Singing the Faith 208	Psalm 147
Mon	2†	Luke 2:15-21	Singing the Faith 358	Psalm 8
Tue	3	Galatians 4:4-7	Singing the Faith 503	Psalm 67
Wed	4	Colossians 1:15-20	Singing the Faith 199	Psalm 98
Thu	5	Isaiah 49:1-13	Singing the Faith 228	Psalm 97
Fri	6∞	Matthew 2:1-12	Singing the Faith 225	Psalm 72
Sat	7	Ephesians 3:1-12	Singing the Faith 227	Psalm 100

** Covenant Sunday † Naming and Circumcision of Jesus, trans. ∞ Epiphany*

Week beginning 8 January
1st in Ordinary Time
The Life-giving Word

Sun	8*	Matthew 3:13-17	Singing the Faith 233	Psalm 29
Mon	9	1 John 1:1-4	Singing the Faith 101	Psalm 7:1-11
Tue	10	1 John 1:5-10	Singing the Faith 397	Psalm 8
Wed	11	1 John 2:1-11	Singing the Faith 366	Psalm 9:1-10
Thu	12	1 John 2:12-17	Singing the Faith 370	Psalm 10:1-12
Fri	13	1 John 2:18-21	Singing the Faith 338	Psalm 11:1-5
Sat	14	1 John 2:22-28	Singing the Faith 636	Psalm 12

** The Baptism of Christ*

Week beginning 15 January
2nd in Ordinary Time
Children of God

Sun	15	John 1:29-42	Singing the Faith 347	Psalm 40
Mon	16	1 John 2:29 – 3:6	Singing the Faith 82	Psalm 86
Tue	17	1 John 3:7-24	Singing the Faith 686	Psalm 87
Wed	18*	1 John 4:1-10	Singing the Faith 742	Psalm 88
Thu	19	1 John 4:11-16	Singing the Faith 620	Psalm 89:1-18
Fri	20	1 John 4:17-21	Singing the Faith 125	Psalm 89:19-32
Sat	21	1 John 5:1-21	Singing the Faith 503	Psalm 90

** Octave of Prayer for Christian Unity begins*

Week beginning 22 January
3rd in Ordinary Time
Returning to the Lord

Sun	22*	Matthew 4:12-23	Singing the Faith 674	Psalm 27
Mon	23	Joel 1:1-20	Singing the Faith 561	Psalm 91
Tue	24	Joel 2:1-17	Singing the Faith 64	Psalm 92
Wed	25†	Galatians 1:11-24	Singing the Faith 450	Psalm 139
Thu	26	Joel 2:18-27	Singing the Faith 94	Psalm 93
Fri	27∞	Joel 2:28-32	Singing the Faith 370	Psalm 94:14-23
Sat	28	Joel 3:1-16	Singing the Faith 190	Psalm 95

** Homeless Sunday † Conversion of Paul, Apostle ∞ Holocaust Memorial Day*

Week beginning 29 January
4th in Ordinary Time
Words and Actions

Sun	29	Matthew 5:1-12	Singing the Faith 245	Psalm 15
Mon	30	James 1:1-11	Singing the Faith 180	Psalm 96
Tue	31	James 1:12-18	Singing the Faith 456	Psalm 97
Wed	1	James 1:19-27	Singing the Faith 668	Psalm 98
Thu	2*	Luke 2:22-32	Singing the Faith 232	Psalm 24
Fri	3	James 2:1-7	Singing the Faith 654	Psalm 99
Sat	4	James 2:8-26	Singing the Faith 249	Psalm 100

** Presentation of Christ in the Temple, Candlemas*

Week beginning 5 February
5th in Ordinary Time
Prayer and Faith

Sun	5	Matthew 5:13-20	Singing the Faith 255	Psalm 112
Mon	6	James 3:1-18	Singing the Faith 93	Psalm 101
Tue	7	James 4:1-12	Singing the Faith 681	Psalm 102:1-11
Wed	8	James 4:13-17	Singing the Faith 611	Psalm 102:12-28
Thu	9	James 5:1-6	Singing the Faith 732	Psalm 103
Fri	10	James 5:7-12	Singing the Faith 203	Psalm 104:1-23
Sat	11	James 5:13-20	Singing the Faith 518	Psalm 104:24-35

Week beginning 12 February

6th in Ordinary Time

Responding to Glory

Sun	12*	Matthew 5:21-37	Singing the Faith 691	Psalm 119:1-8
Mon	13	Ezekiel 1:2-11, 24-28	Singing the Faith 18	Psalm 105:1-15
Tue	14	Ezekiel 2:1-10	Singing the Faith 20	Psalm 106:1-8
Wed	15	Ezekiel 3:1-14	Singing the Faith 32	Psalm 106:43-48
Thu	16	Ezekiel 9:1-4	Singing the Faith 455	Psalm 107:1-16
Fri	17	Ezekiel 10:4-22	Singing the Faith 84	Psalm 107:17-32
Sat	18	Ezekiel 11:14-25	Singing the Faith 545	Psalm 107:33-43

** Racial Justice Sunday*

Week beginning 19 February

7th in Ordinary Time

Judgement and Mercy

Sun	19	Matthew 5:38-48	Singing the Faith 276	Psalm 119:33-40
Mon	20	Ezekiel 14:1-11	Singing the Faith 435	Psalm 110
Tue	21	Ezekiel 15:1-8	Singing the Faith 53	Psalm 111
Wed	22	Ezekiel 16:59-63	Singing the Faith 436	Psalm 112
Thu	23	Ezekiel 17:22-24	Singing the Faith 318	Psalm 113
Fri	24	Ezekiel 20:33-44	Singing the Faith 43	Psalm 114
Sat	25	Ezekiel 33:30-33	Singing the Faith 438	Psalm 115

Week beginning 26 February

Week before Lent

Restoration and Unity

Sun	26	Matthew 17:1-9	Singing the Faith 259	Psalm 99
Mon	27	Ezekiel 34:1-16	Singing the Faith 479	Psalm 116
Tue	28	Ezekiel 34:17-24	Singing the Faith 481	Psalm 117
Wed	1*	Matthew 6:1-6, 16-21	Singing the Faith 236	Psalm 51
Thu	2	Ezekiel 37:1-14	Singing the Faith 386	Psalm 118:1-9
Fri	3†	Ezekiel 37:15-23	Singing the Faith 185	Psalm 118:10-18
Sat	4	Ezekiel 37:14-28	Singing the Faith 350	Psalm 118:19-29

** Ash Wednesday † Women's World Day of Prayer*

Week beginning 5 March

1st in Lent

The Wisdom of the Cross

Sun	5	Matthew 4:1-11	Singing the Faith 235	Psalm 32
Mon	6	1 Corinthians 1:1-9	Singing the Faith 608	Psalm 119:1-16
Tue	7	1 Corinthians 1:18-25	Singing the Faith 455	Psalm 119:17-32
Wed	8	1 Corinthians 1:26-31	Singing the Faith 273	Psalm 119:33-48
Thu	9	1 Corinthians 2:1-5	Singing the Faith 278	Psalm 119:49-64
Fri	10	1 Corinthians 2:6-16	Singing the Faith 153	Psalm 119:65-80
Sat	11	1 Corinthians 3:1-9	Singing the Faith 159	Psalm 119:81-96

Week beginning 12 March

2nd in Lent

Working with One Foundation

Sun	12	John 3:1-17	Singing the Faith 503	Psalm 121
Mon	13	1 Corinthians 3:18-23	Singing the Faith 372	Psalm 119:97-112
Tue	14	1 Corinthians 4:1-5	Singing the Faith 732	Psalm 119:113-128
Wed	15	1 Corinthians 4:6-17	Singing the Faith 458	Psalm 119:129-144
Thu	16	1 Corinthians 5:1-8	Singing the Faith 598	Psalm 119:145-160
Fri	17	1 Corinthians 6:1-11	Singing the Faith 342	Psalm 119:161-176
Sat	18	1 Corinthians 7:25-31	Singing the Faith 633	Psalm 121

Week beginning 19 March

3rd in Lent

Preaching and Example

Sun	19	John 5:5-42	Singing the Faith 556	Psalm 95
Mon	20*	Matthew 1:18-25	Singing the Faith 219	Psalm 89:26-36
Tue	21	1 Corinthians 8:1-8	Singing the Faith 9	Psalm 122
Wed	22	1 Corinthians 8:9-13	Singing the Faith 240	Psalm 123
Thu	23	1 Corinthians 9:15-27	Singing the Faith 634	Psalm 124
Fri	24	1 Corinthians 10:14-22	Singing the Faith 712	Psalm 125
Sat	25†	Luke 1:26-38	Singing the Faith 187	Psalm 40

** Joseph of Nazareth † Annunciation of the Lord*

Week beginning 26 March

4th in Lent

Spiritual Gifts

Sun	26*	Luke 2:33-35	Singing the Faith 119	Psalm 34
Mon	27	1 Corinthians 11:17-22	Singing the Faith 588	Psalm 126
Tue	28	1 Corinthians 11:23-29	Singing the Faith 587	Psalm 127
Wed	29	1 Corinthians 12:1-11	Singing the Faith 593	Psalm 128
Thu	30	1 Corinthians 12:12-26	Singing the Faith 392	Psalm 129
Fri	31	1 Corinthians 12:27-31	Singing the Faith 25	Psalm 130
Sat	1	1 Corinthians 13:1-13	Singing the Faith 242	Psalm 131

** Mothering Sunday*

Week beginning 2 April

Passion Week

Enduring Love

Sun	2	John 11:1-45	Singing the Faith 303	Psalm 130
Mon	3	Song of Solomon 2:1-17	Singing the Faith 269	Psalm 132
Tue	4	Song of Solomon 3:1-5	Singing the Faith 272	Psalm 133
Wed	5	Song of Solomon 5:2-8	Singing the Faith 277	Psalm 134
Thu	6	Song of Solomon 7:10-13	Singing the Faith 279	Psalm 135:1-17
Fri	7	Song of Solomon 8:1-4	Singing the Faith 280	Psalm 135:8-21
Sat	8	Song of Solomon 8:5b-7	Singing the Faith 278	Psalm 136:1-9

Week beginning 9 April

Holy Week

The Way of the Cross

Sun	9	Matthew 27:11-54	Singing the Faith 262	Psalm 31:9-16
Mon	10	John 12:1-11	Singing the Faith 566	Psalm 36
Tue	11	John 12:20-36	Singing the Faith 361	Psalm 71
Wed	12	John 13:21-32	Singing the Faith 421	Psalm 70
Thu	13*	John 13:1-17,31b-35	Singing the Faith 268	Psalm 116
Fri	14†	Isaiah 52:13 – 53:12	Singing the Faith 273	Psalm 22
Sat	15∞	John 19:38-42	Singing the Faith 292	Psalm 4

** Maundy Thursday † Good Friday ∞ Holy Saturday*

Week beginning 16 April

Easter Week

Lord of Life

Sun	16*	Matthew 28:1-10	Singing the Faith 298	Psalm 118
Mon	17	Romans 1:1-7	Singing the Faith 302	Psalm 16
Tue	18	John 5:19-29	Singing the Faith 303	Psalm 33
Wed	19	John 20:1-10	Singing the Faith 309	Psalm 8
Thu	20	Revelation 1:4-8	Singing the Faith 306	Psalm 145
Fri	21	1 Thessalonians 5:1-11	Singing the Faith 304	Psalm 146
Sat	22	John 21:1-14	Singing the Faith 313	Psalm 135

** Easter Day*

Week beginning 23 April

2nd of Easter

The Gospel of the Spirit

Sun	23	John 20:19-31	Singing the Faith 314	Psalm 16
Mon	24	Acts 1:1-8	Singing the Faith 669	Psalm 137:1-7
Tue	25*	Mark 13:5-13	Singing the Faith 154	Psalm 148
Wed	26	Acts 2:1-21	Singing the Faith 372	Psalm 138
Thu	27	Acts 2:14, 22-35	Singing the Faith 285	Psalm 142
Fri	28	Acts 2:36-41	Singing the Faith 419	Psalm 140:1-7
Sat	29	Acts 2:42-47	Singing the Faith 364	Psalm 141:1-5

** Mark, Evangelist*

Week beginning 30 April

3rd of Easter

Apostolic Witness

Sun	30	Luke 24:13-35	Singing the Faith 308	Psalm 116
Mon	1*	John 14:1-14	Singing the Faith 248	Psalm 139
Tue	2	Acts 3:1-10	Singing the Faith 364	Psalm 144
Wed	3	Acts 3:11-19	Singing the Faith 572	Psalm 145:1-7
Thu	4	Acts 4:1-12	Singing the Faith 357	Psalm 145:8-21
Fri	5	Acts 4:13-22	Singing the Faith 345	Psalm 146
Sat	6	Acts 4:23-31	Singing the Faith 682	Psalm 147

** Philip and James, Apostles*

Week beginning 7 May

4th of Easter

Salvation History

Sun	7	John 10:1-10	Singing the Faith 736	Psalm 23
Mon	8	Acts 4:32-35	Singing the Faith 686	Psalm 149:1-5
Tue	9	Acts 5:12-32	Singing the Faith 388	Psalm 150
Wed	10	Acts 7:44-50	Singing the Faith 53	Psalm 1
Thu	11	Acts 7:55-60	Singing the Faith 214	Psalm 2:1-8
Fri	12	Acts 8:14-17	Singing the Faith 395	Psalm 3
Sat	13	Acts 8:26-40	Singing the Faith 385	Psalm 4

Week beginning 14 May

5th of Easter

Sent to the Nations

Sun	14	John 14:1-14	Singing the Faith 252	Psalm 31
Mon	15*	Acts 1:15-26	Singing the Faith 664	Psalm 15
Tue	16	Acts 9:1-20	Singing the Faith 556	Psalm 5:1-8
Wed	17	Acts 9:36-43	Singing the Faith 357	Psalm 6:1-9
Thu	18	Acts 10:34-43	Singing the Faith 348	Psalm 7:1-11
Fri	19	Acts 10:44-48	Singing the Faith 678	Psalm 8
Sat	20	Acts 11:1-18	Singing the Faith 397	Psalm 9:1-10

*Christian Aid Week * Matthias, Apostle, trans.*

Week beginning 21 May

6th of Easter

The Church in Action

Sun	21	John 14:15-21	Singing the Faith 372	Psalm 66
Mon	22	Acts 13:1-12	Singing the Faith 388	Psalm 10:1-12
Tue	23	Acts 13:13-41	Singing the Faith 420	Psalm 11:1-5
Wed	24*	Galatians 4:1-7	Singing the Faith 4	Psalm 130
Thu	25†	Luke 24:44-53	Singing the Faith 300	Psalm 24
Fri	26	Acts 14:8-20	Singing the Faith 727	Psalm 12
Sat	27	Acts 16:1-15	Singing the Faith 493	Psalm 13

** Conversions of John & Charles Wesley † Ascension Day*

Week beginning 28 May

7th of Easter

Captive to the Gospel

Sun	28	John 17:1-11	Singing the Faith 315	Psalm 68
Mon	29	Acts 16:16-34	Singing the Faith 94	Psalm 15
Tue	30	Acts 17:16-34	Singing the Faith 111	Psalm 16
Wed	31*	Luke 1:39-49	Singing the Faith 186	Psalm 113
Thu	1	Acts 18:1-16	Singing the Faith 416	Psalm 17
Fri	2	Acts 19:1-20	Singing the Faith 412	Psalm 18:1-19
Sat	3	Acts 20:17-38	Singing the Faith 692	Psalm 19

** Visitation of Mary to Elizabeth*

Week beginning 4 June

Pentecost

The Gift of the Spirit

Sun	4*	John 20:19-23	Singing the Faith 371	Psalm 104
Mon	5	Joel 2:23-27	Singing the Faith 369	Psalm 18
Tue	6	Romans 5:1-5	Singing the Faith 372	Psalm 33
Wed	7	John 6:44-51	Singing the Faith 373	Psalm 146
Thu	8	Luke 9:1-6	Singing the Faith 378	Psalm 100
Fri	9	Luke 5:17-26	Singing the Faith 381	Psalm 117
Sat	10	Romans 8:22-27	Singing the Faith 383	Psalm 139

** Day of Pentecost*

Week beginning 11 June

Trinity

Holy, Holy, Holy

Sun	11*	Matthew 28:16-20	Singing the Faith 5	Psalm 8
Mon	12†	Acts 11:19-30	Singing the Faith 407	Psalm 112
Tue	13	Isaiah 6:1-8	Singing the Faith 3	Psalm 29
Wed	14	Romans 8:12-17	Singing the Faith 7	Psalm 73
Thu	15	John 16:12-15	Singing the Faith 9	Psalm 93
Fri	16	Revelation 4:1-11	Singing the Faith 13	Psalm 150
Sat	17	Exodus 3:1-15	Singing the Faith 14	Psalm 100

** Trinity Sunday & Methodist Homes Sunday † Barnabas, Apostle, trans.*

Week beginning 18 June

11th in Ordinary Time

The Glory of the Lamb

Sun	18	Matthew 9:35 – 10:8	Singing the Faith 410	Psalm 116
Mon	19	John 1:1-18	Singing the Faith 212	Psalm 20
Tue	20	John 1:35-51	Singing the Faith 350	Psalm 21:1-7
Wed	21	John 2:1-12	Singing the Faith 192	Psalm 22:1-21
Thu	22	John 2:13-25	Singing the Faith 247	Psalm 22:22-31
Fri	23	John 3:1-15	Singing the Faith 16	Psalm 23
Sat	24*	Luke 1:57-66, 80	Singing the Faith 73	Psalm 80:1-7

*World Refugee Week * Birth of John the Baptist*

Week beginning 25 June

12th in Ordinary Time

Living Water

Sun	25	Matthew 10:24-39	Singing the Faith 535	Psalm 86
Mon	26	John 3:16-21	Singing the Faith 59	Psalm 24
Tue	27	John 3:22-30	Singing the Faith 316	Psalm 25
Wed	28	John 3:31-36	Singing the Faith 432	Psalm 26
Thu	29*	Matthew 16:13-19	Singing the Faith 322	Psalm 125
Fri	30	John 4:1-26	Singing the Faith 330	Psalm 27
Sat	1	John 4:27-42	Singing the Faith 566	Psalm 29

** Peter, Apostle*

Week beginning 2 July
13th in Ordinary Time
Sent by the Father

Sun	2	Matthew 10:40-42	Singing the Faith 695	Psalm 89:1-18
Mon	3*	John 20:24-29	Singing the Faith 316	Psalm 31:1-6
Tue	4	John 4:43-54	Singing the Faith 195	Psalm 30
Wed	5	John 5:1-18	Singing the Faith 466	Psalm 31:1-8
Thu	6	John 5:19-29	Singing the Faith 364	Psalm 31:9-24
Fri	7	John 5:30-47	Singing the Faith 55	Psalm 32
Sat	8	John 6:1-15	Singing the Faith 324	Psalm 33

** Thomas, Apostle*

Week beginning 9 July
14th in Ordinary Time
Bread of Life

Sun	9*	Matthew 11:16-19, 25-30	Singing the Faith 322	Psalm 45
Mon	10	John 6:16-29	Singing the Faith 125	Psalm 34:1-10
Tue	11	John 6:30-40	Singing the Faith 713	Psalm 34:11-22
Wed	12	John 6:41-51	Singing the Faith 712	Psalm 35:9-18
Thu	13	John 6:52-59	Singing the Faith 150	Psalm 36
Fri	14	John 6:60-71	Singing the Faith 109	Psalm 38:1-9
Sat	15	John 7:1-13	Singing the Faith 478	Psalm 38:10-22

** Action for Children Sunday*

Week beginning 16 July
15th in Ordinary Time
The New Prophet

Sun	16	Matthew 13:1-9, 18-23	Singing the Faith 671	Psalm 65
Mon	17	John 7:14-24	Singing the Faith 675	Psalm 37:1-11
Tue	18	John 7:25-36	Singing the Faith 12	Psalm 37:12-29
Wed	19	John 7:37-52	Singing the Faith 248	Psalm 37:30-40
Thu	20	John 7:53 – 8:11	Singing the Faith 613	Psalm 119:113-128
Fri	21	John 8:12-20	Singing the Faith 59	Psalm 39
Sat	22*	Luke 8:1-3	Singing the Faith 471	Psalm 63:1-8

** Mary Magdalene*

Week beginning 23 July
16th in Ordinary Time
Honouring the Father

Sun	23	Matthew 13:24-30, 36-43	Singing the Faith 114	Psalm 139
Mon	24	John 8:21-30	Singing the Faith 361	Psalm 40:1-10
Tue	25*	Matthew 20:20-28	Singing the Faith 486	Psalm 126
Wed	26	John 8:31-47	Singing the Faith 485	Psalm 41
Thu	27	John 8:48-59	Singing the Faith 91	Psalm 42
Fri	28	John 9:1-12	Singing the Faith 582	Psalm 43
Sat	29	John 9:13-23	Singing the Faith 440	Psalm 44:1-8

** James, Apostle*

Week beginning 30 July
17th in Ordinary Time
The Shepherd's Glory

Sun	30	Matthew 13:31-33, 44-52	Singing the Faith 412	Psalm 105
Mon	31	John 9:24-41	Singing the Faith 493	Psalm 57
Tue	1	John 10:1-10	Singing the Faith 480	Psalm 46
Wed	2	John 10:11-21	Singing the Faith 537	Psalm 80
Thu	3	John 10:22-42	Singing the Faith 535	Psalm 48
Fri	4	John 11:1-16	Singing the Faith 252	Psalm 49
Sat	5	John 11:17-27	Singing the Faith 370	Psalm 50:1-15

Week beginning 6 August
18th in Ordinary Time
Newness of Life

Sun	6*	Luke 9:28-36	Singing the Faith 261	Psalm 47
Mon	7	John 11:28-37	Singing the Faith 420	Psalm 51
Tue	8	John 11:38-44	Singing the Faith 647	Psalm 52
Wed	9	John 11:45-57	Singing the Faith 492	Psalm 53
Thu	10	John 12:1-11	Singing the Faith 56	Psalm 54
Fri	11	John 12:12-19	Singing the Faith 263	Psalm 55:1-8
Sat	12	John 12:20-50	Singing the Faith 306	Psalm 55:16-22

** The Transfiguration of Christ*

Week beginning 13 August
19th in Ordinary Time
Servant of All

Sun	13	Matthew 14:22-33	Singing the Faith 457	Psalm 85
Mon	14	John 13:1-11	Singing the Faith 249	Psalm 56
Tue	15*	Galatians 4:4-7	Singing the Faith 120	Psalm 45
Wed	16	John 13:12-20	Singing the Faith 244	Psalm 61
Thu	17	John 13:21-30	Singing the Faith 620	Psalm 62
Fri	18	John 13:31-38	Singing the Faith 398	Psalm 63:1-8
Sat	19	John 14:1-14	Singing the Faith 470	Psalm 64

** The Blessed Virgin Mary*

Week beginning 20 August
20th in Ordinary Time
One True Foundation

Sun	20	Matthew 15:21-28	Singing the Faith 251	Psalm 133
Mon	21	John 14:15-17	Singing the Faith 106	Psalm 65
Tue	22	John 14:18-31	Singing the Faith 476	Psalm 66
Wed	23	John 15:1-6	Singing the Faith 389	Psalm 67
Thu	24*	Luke 22:24-30	Singing the Faith 623	Psalm 145
Fri	25	John 15:7-17	Singing the Faith 242	Psalm 68:1-20
Sat	26	John 15:18-26	Singing the Faith 338	Psalm 68:24-35

** Bartholomew, Apostle*

Week beginning 27 August

21st in Ordinary Time

The Work of the Spirit

Sun	27	Matthew 16:13-20	Singing the Faith 601	Psalm 124
Mon	28	John 16:1-7	Singing the Faith 351	Psalm 69:1-21
Tue	29*	Matthew 14:1-12	Singing the Faith 732	Psalm 11
Wed	30	John 16:8-11	Singing the Faith 450	Psalm 69:30-36
Thu	31	John 16:12-15	Singing the Faith 297	Psalm 71:1-14
Fri	1	John 16:16-24	Singing the Faith 76	Psalm 71:15-28
Sat	2	John 16:25-33	Singing the Faith 332	Psalm 75:1-7

** Beheading of John the Baptist*

Week beginning 3 September

22nd in Ordinary Time

Resurrection and Life

Sun	3	Matthew 16:21-28	Singing the Faith 518	Psalm 26
Mon	4	1 Peter 1:1-12	Singing the Faith 345	Psalm 73:1-14
Tue	5	1 Peter 1:13-25	Singing the Faith 361	Psalm 73:15-28
Wed	6	1 Peter 2:1-10	Singing the Faith 456	Psalm 74:1-12
Thu	7	1 Peter 2:11-25	Singing the Faith 278	Psalm 74:13-23
Fri	8*	Micah 5:1-4	Singing the Faith 325	Psalm 45
Sat	9	1 Peter 3:1-12	Singing the Faith 606	Psalm 76

** Nativity of the Virgin Mary*

Week beginning 10 September

23rd in Ordinary Time

The Life of Faith

Sun	10*	Matthew 18:15-20	Singing the Faith 36	Psalm 119:33-40
Mon	11	1 Peter 3:13-22	Singing the Faith 214	Psalm 77
Tue	12	1 Peter 4:1-19	Singing the Faith 520	Psalm 78:1-7
Wed	13	1 Peter 5:1-14	Singing the Faith 493	Psalm 80
Thu	14†	Philippians 2:6-11	Singing the Faith 279	Psalm 22
Fri	15	2 Peter 1:1-15	Singing the Faith 147	Psalm 81
Sat	16	2 Peter 1:16-18	Singing the Faith 155	Psalm 82

** Education Sunday † Holy Cross Day*

Week beginning 17 September

24th in Ordinary Time

The Good Shepherd

Sun	17	Matthew 18:21-35	Singing the Faith 613	Psalm 103
Mon	18	2 Peter 1:19-21	Singing the Faith 155	Psalm 84
Tue	19	2 Peter 3:1-7	Singing the Faith 732	Psalm 85
Wed	20	2 Peter 3:8-10	Singing the Faith 204	Psalm 86
Thu	21*	Matthew 9:9-13	Singing the Faith 653	Psalm 119:65-72
Fri	22	2 Peter 3:11-13	Singing the Faith 205	Psalm 87
Sat	23	2 Peter 3:14-18	Singing the Faith 503	Psalm 88

** Matthew, Apostle and Evangelist*

East Anglia District

Chair
Julian Pursehouse

Cromer Beach
(Julian Pursehouse)

We give thanks for the faithful resilience of presbyters and deacons across the East Anglia District;
for school chaplains who bring a Christian presence to Culford School and the Leys School;
for the work among homeless and socially deprived people at Cromer Methodist Church;
for the imaginative reconfiguration of the premises at Wicken Methodist Church in the Ely and Newmarket Circuit.
We pray for the newly constituted District Mentoring Group which offers support and mentoring to presbyters and deacons;
for the many lay employees across the District who serve God in many different ways;
for those who are reimagining rural presence and ministry;
for members of the Eastern Region DMLN Team;
for the regional study days shared with the Bedfordshire, Essex and Hertfordshire District.

Praying with depression
I cannot pray; the past is too painful for praise,
the future is too frightening for hope.
I am frozen in the present – black, unending.

My precious child, how you feel now will pass,
and though you cannot discern it,
my love tenderly surrounds you.
I will not let you go.

Naomi Sharp, Huddersfield

Life-giving God, in whose presence there is an abundance of hope and a plenitude of grace, grant that we may build communities of hospitality where bread is shared, forgiveness offered and justice proclaimed. And so, as our life together is shaped by your love, give us the grace to share the freedom that is ours in Christ, that others may taste and see the goodness of your kingdom. Amen.

Julian Pursehouse, East Anglia District Chair

Dear Lord, please wrap your warm, loving arms around our world.
Please protect the people in the world who are suffering great loss and grief.
Please keep all your children safe and protected
from wars, famine, natural disasters and plagues.
Please help the world look for the good, and banish bad and evil.
May they not give up hope, in the name of Jesus Christ. Amen.

Erin Finch, Year 6, Bedford Hall Methodist Primary School, Wigan

DAY 15

Praying with Christians in the Middle East

Middle East Council of Churches

Iran

Syria

Lebanon

Egypt

Israel/Palestine

Mission Partner
John Howard° (sd)

EAPPI (Ecumenical Accompaniment Programme in Palestine and Israel)
Katherine Fox

The separation barrier in Bethlehem (John Howard)

Take our bodies, O Christ, to do your work; for here on earth you have no body now but ours. Take our hands to be your hands, and our feet to walk in the ways of your feet. Take our eyes to be the eyes of your own compassion, shining out in a troubled world; for your own mercies' sake. Amen.

Teresa of Avila (1515-1582)

Lord Jesus, you came as the Prince of Peace. We pray for peace in the troubled **Middle East**, and especially for **Israel/ Palestine**. May the Jerusalem office of the Methodist Church be a community of peacemakers, breaking down walls and barriers of fear, suspicion and greed. May the staff and volunteers be dedicated to building up the relationships between peace-loving people in both Israel and Palestine. Grant us safety and courage as we seek to follow the ways of justice and peace. Amen.

John Howard, mission partner, Israel/Palestine

Break down the wall, O God,
break down the dividing wall.
Be our peace and make us one:
one group, one family, one people:
Muslim, Christian and Jew,
together and free in you. Amen.
Based on Ephesians 2:14

Elspeth Strachan, EAPPI

With us God, you came to share our human lives
in Bethlehem, 'the house of bread'.
We pray for those who bake bread and break it
on both sides of the wall of separation:
Jewish families gathered for the Shabbat meal,
Christian and Muslim Palestinians,
sharing flatbread fresh from the taboun.
You are living bread, broken that all might be fully alive,
so we pray for the day when all your children
will be free to share their daily bread together, in peace. Amen.

Jan Sutch Pickard, Iona Community

EAPPI are always looking for volunteer human rights monitors to help put prayers for a just peace in Israel-Palestine into action.
For more information please visit www.quaker.org.uk/eappi

Isle of Man District

Rheynn Ellan Vannin Yn Agglish Haasilagh

Chair
Richard Hall

Traditional Manx Cottage, Cregneash Heritage Village (Richard Hall)

We give thanks for the completion of the building work at Ballagarey and the ongoing and developing life of this centre for prayer;
for those who have committed to the new worship leaders training course and all those who have been involved in the Mission Shaped Introduction course in recent months;
for the stationing process, through which two new presbyters have been added to the team on the island.
We pray for the courage to continue to embrace change and growth in all its forms as the District seeks to be relevant to the needs of those it serves;
for the newly-formed sections on the island and those who minister through them;
for the ongoing process of regrouping and discernment of God's vision for the District's future ministry;
for those who have joined the district staff team this year and those who continue faithfully to serve the Church there.

Lord, help us to share the good things you have given us in our life together with those who need to know that they are loved and valued. We offer this day to you; those we will meet along the way who need our help and support; and those who will minister to us. And we pray that you will bless the communities that we serve. Amen.

Richard Hall, Isle of Man District Chair

Loving and compassionate God, we thank you that, in Jesus, we see your care and concern for all people in action.
We pray that we may follow your example and, through your Holy Spirit, we may offer that love to others, especially those in need. We pause to reflect on the people and situations that those words bring to mind. We remember in particular the Leaders of Worship and Preachers Homes, the four 'Westerleys', that offer residential care to those who can no longer live independently. We ask your blessing on the residents, and on those who care for them.
Our prayers, though the Leaders and Worship and Preachers Trust, go to all those who preach, speaking to people according to their needs, that their acts of worship, and the example of their lives, may sustain, comfort and challenge those who hear them. Amen.

Joyce Pipet, former trustee, LWPT

DAY 16

Praying with Christians in the Indian Subcontinent

Be light, O Lord, to our eyes, music to our ears and contentment to our heart. Be sunlight in our day, food at our table and rest to us in the night. Let us rejoice to be about your business and let us live to your praise and glory, now and for ever. Amen.

John Cosin (1594-1672)

Church of Pakistan

Moderator
Sammy Azariah

Mission Partner
Rachel Ullmer (ed)

Scholarship Students
Evelyn Bhajan
Souniel Mehboob
(both in Britain)

Church of Bangladesh

Moderator
Paul Sarkar

Women's lIteracy group in Lahore (Ayra Indryas)

We give thanks for the literacy project of the Women's Desk of the Church of **Pakistan** in the Lahore Diocese which aims to equip and empower people (mostly women but also some men) in different ways, including through adult literacy classes.
We pray that many illiterate adults will gain an education which will help them to set up businesses and support their families; for the 11 women and 3 men who have been trained as literacy trainers, that they may help many more to read and to improve their skills.

Information supplied by the World Church Relationships Office

We give thanks for a positive attitude from the government of Pakistan towards protecting schools;
for the care given by teachers to the children in school;
for the dedication of many Pakistani Christians working with the poor in difficult conditions.
We pray for the safety of pupils and schools in Pakistan;
for the implementation of Bible curricula in schools;
for the work of Sunday Schools with young people.

Rachel Ullmer, mission partner, Pakistan

We pray for **Bangladesh**, a land of beauty, vibrancy and diversity, yet where poverty and unemployment is rife. The Church of Bangladesh works alongside communities to assist the vulnerable, the marginalised and the oppressed, through development programmes, towards resilient livelihoods, food security, community health and nutrition, gender justice, women's empowerment and children's rights.
As the Church shares Christian love with children through the many schools and hostels, technical workshops, women's groups, Sunday Schools and community churches, we pray that they may all know and feel they belong to a wider community.

Pat Jamison, former mission partner, Bangladesh, now serving in Ghana

Belfast District (Ireland)

Superintendent
Thomas McKnight

We give thanks for the work of the Methodist missions in Central and East Belfast;
for growth and outreach in an increasingly secularised city, particularly with the Sandy Row congregation;
for a growing realisation within the District of the oneness of God's mission, with recent district mission services combining focus on both world and home mission.
We pray for both sides of the still-divided city of Belfast, as its people find ways to deal with the hurts of the past;
for the Pioneer Mission ministry of Well.com at Carlisle Circus, which provides a professional psychological service and spiritual direction in one of the most deprived areas of Belfast.

Leeds District

Chair
Anne Brown

We offer thanks for the diversity of human experience and culture within the communities served by the Leeds District;
for public spaces – parks, sports centres, libraries, galleries and arts venues – that enrich and strengthen the communal fabric of those living in the District.
We pray for those who give freely of their time and skills to ensure that strangers – students, refugees, young workers and families – are welcomed in communities where they can live in safety and with mutual respect;
for partnerships in the urban centres of Leeds, Wakefield, Harrogate, Pontefract and Castleford, and for the hospitality offered by churches.

Holy Wisdom,
free us to participate more deeply
in the divine dance of creating, redeeming
and healing our world.

Liberating God,
release in us a passionate energy
for seeking justice;
for investing in peace;
for tending the needs of fragile human communities;
for befriending and healing the planet.

Companion at the well,
help us to draw and to share fresh clean water,
for the health of our bodies, the clarity of our thinking.
and the wholeness of our soul-making. Amen.

Liz Smith, former Leeds District Chair

View from the Chevin, Otley (Liz Smith)

DAY 17

Praying with Christians in India

Church of North India (CNI)

Moderator
P K Samantaroy

Scholarship Student
Sanjana Das Singh
(in South Africa)

Church of South India (CSI)

Moderator
G Devakadasham

Scholarship Student
Paul Singh Job Retnaselvam
(in Britain)

Dr Jill Barber sharing family stories with Rita Devi at an All We Can project in North India (Laura Cook, All We Can)

Let the door of our heart be opened to receive Christ, our Lord and our God. Let the soul of our being be unlocked, to welcome our Saviour, the Redeemer of all. Let the gates of our life be flung wide, for the entering in of the Sun of Righteousness, even the King of Glory. Amen.

Ambrose of Milan (c. 334-397)

We give thanks for all the partners who support the Church of North **India** in its various programmes, reaching out to the most vulnerable and deprived communities across India.
We pray for the leadership of the Church of North India and for all the region's bishops and presbyters;
for the Mission Evangelism Triennium, a programme of evangelism which is bringing mission programmes and gospel conventions to all 27 dioceses of the Church of North India;
for PDS* Hostels for needy children;
for work with women, dalit and other marginalised people.

Alwan Masih, General Secretary, Church of North India Synod

We give thanks for the partnership between Methodist Women in Britain and the Church of North India (CNI), which is bringing mutual learning, prayer and support;
for the Easter Offering Service 2016 which highlighted, across the Methodist Church in Britain, work being done to bring freedoms to the marginalised and excluded members of CNI;
We pray for minds to be opened and attitudes to be changed towards the dalit people of India;
for women everywhere to be freed and empowered to achieve their God-given potential.

Linda Crossley, former Vice-President, Methodist Women in Britain

Glorious God, we thank you for India and for the lives that are being improved through All We Can's partners. We praise you for the families who have been reconciled, the marginalised who have been given a place in society and for the women who are taking more control over their lives. We ask for your wisdom to equip those who are finding solutions to the problems that surround them. May the afflicted know peace, the hungry receive food, the oppressed be granted justice and the broken-hearted experience joy and hope. Amen.

Rebecca Branch, All We Can

PDS = Parent, Diocese, Synod, where one third of the cost is met by each party to enable poorer children to attend good schools

Lincolnshire District

Chair
Bruce Thompson

Lincoln Cathedral
(Bruce Thompson)

We give thanks for places of learning across Lincolnshire;
for the two universities within Lincoln,
for the colleges of higher and further education, schools, academies, nurseries and training centres.
We pray for the joint Methodist-Anglican Schools of Brant Broughton, Bardney, New Holland, Caistor and the Magdalen Academy at Wainfleet, for their headteachers, staff and pupils.

We pray for all those who carry the privilege and responsibility of nurturing, instructing and developing children and young people. We ask that they may be fully aware of the appreciation and respect within which they are held by those of us who acknowledge their gifts and commitment.
We hold before God all who read, study and reflect upon the Scriptures, theological and spiritual works, that they may find inspiration, renewal and a deepening and broadening understanding of the faith to which they hold.
We give thanks for those who taught us about the things we now cherish. May we recognise the impact they have had upon our lives and the difference we made to the world about us.
May we recognise the duties to which we are called in passing on the truths of the gospel and the tools for living out that gospel.

Bruce Thompson, Lincolnshire District Chair

We rely upon you, O God,
to be our companion when others are nowhere to be found.
We call upon you O God,
to be a voice when we struggle to find the words we need.
We rest upon you O God,
our haven when the walls of life close in on us.
For the times when we are alone,
or silenced by the moment,
or crushed by the weight,
we look to you, O God, our companion, voice and haven.
In the gatherings, noise and expanse,
may we never forget that you remain an ever-constant presence,
the God of life, liberation and love. Amen.

Bruce Thompson, Lincolnshire District Chair

DAY 18

Praying with Christians in Asia

Teach us, O Lord, to attempt what we fear we cannot attain, to ascend what we fear we cannot reach and to express what we fear we cannot utter. In adoring you whom we cannot comprehend, teach us to celebrate the faith we cannot prove; for your own love's sake. Amen.

Hilary of Poitiers (315-367)

The Methodist Church of Upper Myanmar

Methodist President
James Ngun Hlei

Scholarship Students
Fung Mang
Lal Rin Sanga
San Pwint
(all in The Philippines)
Van Lal Thuam Lian
(in Britain)
Van Lal Mal Sawma
(in USA)
Yaw Ling
Thla Sung
(both in Japan)
Sui Lian Thang
(in Hong Kong)

We give thanks for successful and peaceful national elections in Myanmar in 2015;
for international partners who join in the work of the Church in Myanmar;
for the never-failing guidance of God through the years.
We pray for a dedicated office building to support the work of the Methodist Church in Upper Myanmar which has been undertaking its mission for over 100 years without adequate accommodation;
for the unity of all Wesleyan churches in Myanmar;
for true religious freedom for Christians in the Buddhist-dominated culture of Myanmar;
for positive changes in Myanmar under Aung San Suu Kyi's NLD-led government, after 50 years of military dictatorship.

James Ngun Hlei, President, Methodist Church of Upper Myanmar

The United Mission to Nepal (UMN)

Director of the UMN
Joel Hafvenstein

Scholarship Student
Shrina Maharjan Subedi (in Britain)

We pray for the four special groups of people identified by the United Mission to Nepal as being most in need of support.

We pray for freedom for women;
freedom from violence, exploitation and fear,
freedom to choose, to love, and to raise their children in safety.

We pray for freedom for children;
freedom from work and from want,
freedom to play, to learn and to be kids.

We pray for freedom for people with disabilities;
freedom from discrimination, loneliness and frustration,
freedom to live as others do in the community.

We pray for freedom for people of low caste;
freedom from poverty and powerlessness,
freedom to participate and to live with dignity. Amen.

Lyn Jackson, Communications Director, United Mission to Nepal

Liverpool District

Chair
Sheryl Anderson

We give thanks for the lives of witness and service, and for the projects and ministries in the Liverpool District that seek to share those possibilities with everyone;
for work with asylum seekers and refugees carried out through Churches Together in the Merseyside Region and beyond;
for the Liverpool Council of Faiths, demonstrating solidarity for Liverpool's many diverse and distinct faith communities;
We pray for the growing work with schools, particularly through 'Hope Journey' events;
for chaplaincies in higher education, hospitals and prisons;
for all the Methodist-sponsored lunch clubs, foodbanks, coffee mornings, supper clubs, cafés, and bread-making activities, that offer welcome, acceptance, safety, and friendship to those with fragile lives;
and especially for the unique ministry of hope offered to survivors of abuse through the careful and caring work of the Church Action on Sexual Abuse Issues.

God our Father, it is your will that all people should live together in harmony and liberty, free from want and war, from exploitation and oppression, from false doctrines and false gods and from the guilt and power of sin. We thank you for your servants, past and present, who have worked and fought and suffered in the cause of freedom. Give us grace that we too may work in the service of your kingdom on earth. Make us vigilant, bold and active in promoting and protecting every kind of freedom, wherever it is denied or threatened. We pray in the name of Jesus who for our freedom took the form of a slave. Amen.

Colin V Smith, supernumerary minister, Sankey Valley Circuit

Who for our freedom took the form of a slave (© Anya Goldsack, used with permission)

Warm, loving Spirit of God;
open our ears, that we may listen in order to understand, not simply to reply;
open our minds, that we may receive new insights into the nature of your love;
and open our hearts, that we may share generously the gifts of your grace.
Thus will we truly be disciples of Jesus Christ, and know the truth,
the truth that will set us free. Amen.

Sheryl Anderson, Liverpool District Chair

DAY 19

Praying with Christians in Asia

In prayer, may we come to know ourselves and to meet our maker; to rejoice in God's goodness, to share in God's life, and to be enfolded in God's love. Amen.

Julian of Norwich (1342-1420)

Indonesia

Methodist Bishop
Darwis Manurung

Sri Lanka

Methodist President
Asiri Perera

Mission Partners
Angleenaº Keizer (p)
Raing and Mervyn McCullagh (sd)

Scholarship Students
James Gnararuban (in Britain)
J. Anpurajah (in Sri Lanka)
Yeherome Michael Wanniyabandara (in Japan)

Kubiendhra and Kulathaiabel, ex-fighters with a peaceful purpose in life.

We pray for the people of **Sri Lanka**, a country which has suffered prolonged ethnic conflict, followed by an horrific 30-year war.
We give thanks that the National Christian Council of Sri Lanka (NCC), in partnership with South African NGO the Institute for Healing of Memories (IHOM), has begun to make safe and sacred spaces so that Sri Lankans may share their stories.
We pray that those who have suffered will find an audience, and embark on a journey of healing.
We pray for Kubiendhra and Kulathaiabel, who were fighters in the civil war, and give thanks that the Methodist Church has helped them set up a business repairing computers and mobile phones, which has enabled them to move on from hatred and resentment and given them a peaceful purpose in life.

Information supplied by the World Church Relationships Office

We give thanks for the work over the last five years for the work of Lakshman Rosa (NMA) as an inter-faith officer with the Methodist Church Sri Lanka, working with other faiths to help solve local issues, a sign of great hope in Sri Lanka's post-conflict situation.
We pray for farmers in Anaradhapura where there is a high incidence of kidney disease caused by agricultural chemicals, that screening clinics will provide appropriate treatments.

Information supplied by the World Church Relationships Office

Loving, merciful God, we pray for the refugees; many have no idea where they are going, but we ask that they will find a place where they can settle, find work and education for their children. At the end of their journeys may they find love and peace and freedom from all fear and suffering. We pray for all who feel they have all they want, far more than they need, and yet have no consideration for others. Open their eyes and ears, Lord, to the cries of all those suffering people, so that they will learn to show real compassion and concern. In the name of him who suffered for all, Jesus our Lord and Saviour. Amen.

June Dingwall, local preacher, Exeter Coast and Country Circuit

Manchester and Stockport District

Chair
Andrew Lunn

The glorious freedom of the children of God (Ward Jones)

We give thanks for the freedom we find in one another, as we are united in Christ and through the Holy Spirit;
for the situations in which Methodist people feel supported and encouraged by a sense of connexion;
for the growing fresh expressions of church within the Manchester and Stockport District, and the freedom found within them to worship and serve you in new and living ways.
We pray for The Welcome in Knutsford, Sanctus in central Manchester, The Community in Marple, Salt Cellar in Oldham and The Chapel in the Fields at Sinderland;
for churches within the District which help refugees and those seeking sanctuary, including Emmanuel Community Centre in Salford, and Long Street Methodist Church in Middleton;
for the hospitality offered through the work of Methodist International House in Manchester.
for the new district development plan, that the people of the District will be encouraged to build on our ecumenical, community, and World Church links.

Gracious God we thank you,
for we find freedom in life,
and freedom in death;
freedom in receiving you,
and freedom in giving to others.

May we live bold and Godly lives,
and set captives free in your name,
so that all will proclaim their freedom in Christ. Amen.

Craig Gaffney, Methodist Youth President, 2015/2016

Liberating Lord,
under the burden of your cross you walked free of constraint;
and by your resurrection you lead us into the glorious freedom of the children of God.
As you free us from fear, let us live out your love;
as you free us from anxiety, let us live in your joy;
as you free us from hatred, let us live in your peace;
as you free us from shortness of temper, let us live with your patience;
as you free us from callousness, let us live by your kindness;
as you free us from greed, let us live with your goodness;
as you free us from violent impulse, let us live with your gentleness;
as you free us from inconstancy, let us live through your faithfulness;
as you free us from disobedience, let us live in your self-control. Amen.

Andrew Lunn, Manchester and Stockport District Chair

DAY 20

Praying with Christians in Asia

God the Father, eternally mysterious, we worship you. God the Son, eternally responding, we bless you. God the Holy Spirit, eternally witnessing, we adore you. Holy and glorious Trinity, three persons and one God, we magnify you, now and for ever. Amen.

Nestorian Liturgy (5th century)

Singapore

Methodist Bishop
Wee Boon Hup

Malaysia

Methodist Bishop
Ong Hwai Teik

Vietnam

Mission Partner
Eden° Fletcher (ed)
(+UMC)

We give thanks that the Methodist Church in **Singapore** is blessed with members who are not only faithful in their witness, but also active in their contribution to society, both in the public and private sectors;
for the active role the Church has played in establishing Methodist missions in seven countries in the region.
We pray for a harmonious relationship among the various faith groups in Singapore;
for young Muslims who are at risk of radicalisation through the online influence of ISIS;
for future generations of Methodists, that they may be spiritually grounded, as well as socially and missionally active, as they play their part in the Church and in society.

Wee Boon Hup, Bishop, Methodist Church in Singapore

We give thanks that the Church in Sarawak, East **Malaysia**, has freedom to share its faith in that land; may this freedom prevail. We pray also that the freedom to share Christian values in Methodist Primary and Middle Schools will continue to influence people of different racial and social backgrounds, and build bridges of tolerance and understanding. We pray for the Theological School in Sibu as it trains Chinese- and Iban-speaking students for both lay and ordained ministry;
that teachers and students may be granted the wisdom to share your truth with love and sensitivity in Malaysia's multi-cultural society.

Geoffrey Senior, former mission partner, Malaysia

Dearest Lord,
I thank you for today of all days.
How happy I am that you have held
this time and place for me in your dear heart.
God of blessings, I praise you. Amen.

Hazel Stagg, local preacher and Pastoral Community Worker, Banbury Circuit

God of blessings, I praise you (Maree Farrimond)

Newcastle upon Tyne District

Chair
Stephen Lindridge

© Christmas Angels, used with permission

We give thanks for lives touched and blessed through the 20,000 knitted angels distributed at Christmas 2015 throughout the Newcastle District;
for new faith in Christ arising from the Together Mission and the many volunteers who grew in their own discipleship by participating in this week of service and outreach.
We pray for those in the District who have lost their homes in floods and storms, and for provision where insurance will not cover what is lost;
for lay and ordained people within the District, that they may build each other up in a genuine community that fruitfully shows to the world the practical, tangible love of God;
for the young people whose lives have been touched by 3Generate, ECG, Soul Survivor and similar initiatives within the District – may their love of Jesus equip them to hear God's call.

Thank you, Lord, for your passion shown to us in the servant Christ. We praise you, Holy Spirit, for stirring, calling and inspiring us to engage with you in renewing your Church to be fit for your purpose to serve the present age. Give us wisdom and courage to let go of those things that are barriers to fruitfulness. Bless those who, with integrity, find comfort in past ways. Help us to meet each others' needs with love, grace and respect. Fill us all with your Spirit, that we might be Jesus to our families, friends and neighbours. May all that we do be about Jesus and making his Church fruitful. Amen.

Tim Thorpe, superintendent minister, Newcastle West Circuit

Gracious God, may Christ be my light though all else fails,
Christ be my hope when doubt is strong,
Christ be my peace when pain is real,
Christ be my love when anger burns,
Christ be my strength when praise is weak,
Christ be the glory when honour is given,
Christ be praised when the kingdom comes,
Christ be the purpose of all our deeds,
Christ be the welcome we give to the stranger,
Christ be the object of our seeking and learning,
Christ be the word on our mouths
at the dawn and close of day. Amen.

Stephen Lindridge, Newcastle District Chair

DAY 21

Praying with Christians in East Asia

Come source of eternal Light. Come giver of eternal Life. Fill our hearts with your love, fill our mouths with your praise and fill our lives with your presence; now and for ever. Amen.

Symeon the New Theologian (949-1022)

China

President of China Christian Council
Gao Feng

Amity Foundation General Secretary
Qiu Zhonghui
Amity is a Chinese non-government organisation founded by Christians.

Hong Kong
(Special Administrative Region of China)

Methodist President
Sung Che Lam

Mission Partners (until November 2016)
Howard° and Rosie Mellor (p/ed)

Bibles for all
(Howard Mellor)

It has often been said that 'History belongs to the intercessors'.
Across the UK, there are many Chinese students.
We pray that the mercy of our Lord may reach them and enter their hearts. May the love of Jesus comfort those who are studying here when they feel homesick and lonely.
May prayer be the cornerstone of all we do. We pray for the Chinese students studying in the UK today:
we share faith's journey with them;
we share Christ's love with them.
May they have joy through their university and church life.
May they encounter Christ while far from home during their endeavours.
May we walk in companionship with them.
May the light shine on their face when they meet Christ. Amen.

Lawrence Law, North-East Chinese Mission Presbyter

We rejoice that in 2015, the Union of Methodists in Hong Kong celebrated the 40th anniversary of its foundation.
We give thanks for the commitment of the Methodist Church in Hong Kong to an integrated mission of evangelism, pastoral care, school education and social service;
that the new Methodist International Church and Conference Building is under construction;
for the ministry of Howard and Rosie Mellor and pray that a suitable successor as superintendent minister will be found.
We pray for good governance in Hong Kong, and for the many people who feel fear, distress and anger about the apparent interference of Beijing in the affairs of Hong Kong;
for the nurturing of civic values such as righteousness, freedom, democracy, rule of law and mutual respect;
for the resolving of the deep-rooted conflicts between the Hong Kong Special Administrative Region and the China mainland, and those within Hong Kong society.

Howard Mellor, former superintendent minister, Methodist International Church, Hong Kong

Down District (Ireland)

Superintendent
Andrew Kingston

We give thanks for community engagement across the Down District through foodbanks and other initiatives;
for training and resources such as Life on the Frontline.
We pray for the leadership training days being held for probationary ministers in the District.

> Sovereign Lord, we give thanks for your servant Patrick who came as a missionary from Britain to Ireland. We give you thanks for your servant Colombanus who, 150 years later, left the mostly Christian island to take the gospel to the European mainland where Christianity was in serious decline. Thank you for the inspiration and the challenge of those who have gone before us. Amen.
>
> *Andrew Kingston, Down District Superintendent*

Lancashire District

Chair
Paul Davis

We give thanks for the covenant partnership across the North West and Mann Region and for sharing in the learning network;
for refurbished buildings in Clitheroe and Padiham Road, Burnley and for the way they have enabled congregations better to serve their communities and to share their faith.
We pray for ARC (the Asylum and Refugee Community) in Blackburn, and the Comfort Zone, providing support to the homeless in Blackpool;
for projects with Methodist Action North West and the work with those in the third age in Lytham St Annes;
for the work that continues to help individuals and communities after their lives have been disrupted by floods in Whalley and the Ribble Valley.

> Gracious God, you give us everything we have
> and everything we take for granted.
> Help us to share the good news with all we meet.
>
> In the knowledge of the gospel,
> may we welcome those seeking asylum and refuge,
> help feed, clothe and shelter those who have nothing,
> uphold those whose abilities have diminished with age,
> and support lives affected
> long after flood waters have disappeared.
> In Christ's name we live and pray. Amen.
>
> *Paul Davis, Lancashire District Chair*

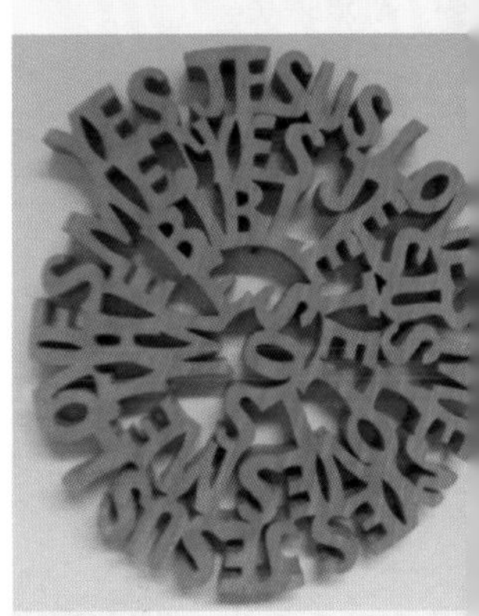

Yes, Jesus loves me, for the Bible tells me so. Wood working by Bob Mayor (Paul Davis)

DAY 22

Praying with Christians in East Asia

O consuming fire, O Spirit of love, descend into the depth of our hearts and there transform us until we are fire of your fire, love of your love, and Christ himself is formed within us. Amen.

Elizabeth of Schonau (d. 1184)

South Korea

Presiding Bishop
Yong-Jai Jun

North Korea

Chair
Kang Myong Chol

Mission Partners
Steve° and Lorraine Emery-Wright (ed)

United Church of Christ in Japan

Moderator
Hideo Ishibashi

Mission Partner
Sheila Norris (ed)

Manager of Bongsoo Church Bakery, Korea (Steve Pearce)

We give thanks for the 130th anniversary of the Methodist mission in **Korea**, remembering the work of the first missionaries and early believers, and renewing their spiritual heritage;
for the 70th year since Korea was liberated from Japanese colonisation in 1945, and the role of the Korean Methodist Church in the struggle for national independence.
We pray for peace and reconciliation in the Korean peninsula at a time of rising tension between the two divided Koreas;
for renewed church membership when congregations are shrinking due to Korea having the world's lowest birth rate;
for the mission partners of the Korean Methodist Church across 78 countries, and for 181 Korean Methodist diaspora churches in 36 countries, that they may serve the kingdom of God to the ends of the earth.

Susan Nam, General Board of Missions, Korean Methodist Church

We give thanks for the quiet daily witness of Christians in **Japan**, who are different in a country where it is much more acceptable to be the same;
for those whose confidence in you gives them the strength to speak out for the values of your kingdom;
for social justice within Japan.
We pray for wisdom in international relations in East Asia, where tensions over territory and resources are growing;
that the voice of the Church in Japan may be strengthened;
that all Japanese Christians may have the grace to wait upon you, the patience to seek your timing to give the word of witness, the courage to speak out for justice, and the assurance of the power of your love.

Sheila Norris, mission partner, Japan

Where the past binds us, Lord, open our hearts to your future.
Where prejudice blinds us, Lord, open our eyes in your love.
Where change frightens us, Lord, give us the courage to care.
Amen.

Thomas McKnight, Belfast District Superintendent

Nottingham and Derby District

Chair
Loraine Mellor

We give thanks for shared initiatives with other Churches and other faiths across the Nottingham and Derby District;
for the partnership with Hope Nottingham, running foodbanks and helping people to find employment;
for the Rushcliffe Memory Café at West Bridgford and the luncheon club at St John's Sutton.
We pray for Support for Refugees, which is run through the work of the citizens' organisations in Nottingham and Mansfield, and for Safe Families for Children;
for initiatives in faith-sharing, such as Messy Churches, the Basement Zone for young people at Phoenix Farm and the 'Garden City' church in the Nottingham East Circuit;
for the Fresh Expressions Pioneer Enabler, and the many initiatives around the District where the gospel is shared.

Lord, in your suffering world, this is our prayer:
for those whose lives have been damaged; for those who know pain and despair in The Meadows, St Anne's, Bestwood Park and Lenton, for those whose lives have crumbled around them in Belper, Coalville and Burton on Trent; for those who don't know how to pick up the pieces of shattered lives in Derby, Alfreton, Hawtonville, Grantham, Ashbourne and Swadlincote. We pray that all may know your love, your grace and in their beauty and brokenness know your brokenness, remembering that you gave up your only Son for us all. Amen.
Loraine Mellor, Nottingham and Derby District Chair

Lord, you have revealed yourself to your people in every generation and invited them to share in the building up of your kingdom. So we pray for the rich heritage of Methodism throughout the British Isles and around the world. We pray for all those historic Methodist churches and other buildings, which exercise a ministry of welcome and hospitality to visitors every day of the year. We pray for all those volunteers who give their time freely to welcome visitors, listen to their joys and sorrows, introduce them to our history and share stories of God's faithful people. We pray for the heritage stewards at Wesley's Chapel in London that they may be enabled to draw people into a deeper encounter with the faith that we profess. In the name of Christ, we pray. Amen.
Jennifer Potter, minister, Wesley's Chapel, London

DAY 23

Praying with Christians in Australia and New Zealand

Power of God, be our protection; wisdom of God, be our guide; word of God, be our inspiration; shield of God, be our defence; hosts of God, be our deliverance; Son of God, be our salvation; now and always. Amen.

St Patrick's Breastplate, Book of Armagh (9th century)

The Uniting Church in Australia

President
Stuart McMillan

Aotearoa / New Zealand

Methodist President
Prince Devanandan
(from October 2016)

We give thanks for the life of the Uniting Church in **Australia** expressed in worship, witness and service;
for the 12 national conferences (the largest being the Tongan and Korean conferences), which are part of the multicultural nature of the Uniting Church;
for the extensive community work done through UnitingCare, the largest NGO providing such services in Australia.
We pray for the congregations across the continent of Australia from large cities to small remote communities;
for UnitingWorld as it connects with Partner Churches in the Pacific, Asia and Africa;
for UnitingJustice especially as it advocates for Christ's compassion to be shown to refugees and asylum seekers;
for the Uniting Aboriginal and Islander Christian Congress as it seeks to foster younger leaders;
for the Uniting Church to be effective and faithful in an increasingly secular context.

Chris Walker, National Consultant, Christian Unity, Doctrine and Worship, Uniting Church in Australia

Australian and Samoan colleagues gathered for an ecumenical service (Uniting Church in Australia)

We give thanks for the opening of two churches in **New Zealand** after earthquake repairs and rebuilding, with two more churches almost completed;
for the inauguration of the National Dialogue for Christian Unity between the Methodist, Roman Catholic and Anglican Churches, with Salvation Army and Presbyterian observers;
for Trinity Methodist Theological College having received government approval and accreditation to teach the NZ Diploma in Christian Studies.
We pray for the completion of the rebuilt Connexional Office after the Christchurch earthquakes;
for the new lay Ministry Support Team, that they may effectively equip and encourage leaders in local congregations;
for the private students enrolled with the Theological College.

David Bush, General Secretary, Methodist Church of New Zealand

Northampton District

Chair
Peter Hancock

We give thanks for the officers, committee members and all those who enable the mission of God through the District;
for the work of the District Director of Mission, Executive Officer for Safeguarding and District Administrators in supporting circuits, churches and individuals;
for the good number of deacons in the District who exercise a variety of mission-shaped ministries;
for the increasing presence of the World Church among us.
We pray for the many churches in rural areas as they seek to sustain a vibrant Christian presence, worshipping God and serving their local communities;
for the witness of the Church in the many areas of the District where large housing developments are planned and under way;
for those churches putting much work into building schemes, that these may enhance their mission.

We give thanks for the resurrection power of Jesus, that no tomb can withstand and no enslavement restrain.
We pray that those under political, economic, social and cultural oppression may experience liberation through the grace of God, the acts of leaders of goodwill and the sacrificial mission of the Church in all parts of the world.
We pray that we, as disciples, may have the courage to let go of our instincts of self-preservation and, in doing so, find the true freedom reserved for those who take up their cross and follow Jesus, the saviour of the world.

Peter Hancock, Northampton District Chair

The resurrection power of Jesus (© Anya Goldsack, used with permission)

Loving God, you have set us free in Christ Jesus!
As we stand in the liberty wherein you have made us free,
enable your Church, through prayer and action,
to share this freedom with all who are:
 oppressed by rulers, structures and systems;
 marginalised because of race, gender, sexuality or
  economic status;
 bound by habits which imprison and degrade;
 silenced because they stand by their faith and for truth,
until all experience life in all its fullness
and the truth which sets all people free. Amen.

Olufemi Cole-Njie,
superintendent minister, Forest Circuit.

DAY 24

Praying with Christians in the Pacific

United Church of the Solomon Islands

Moderator
Wilfred Kurepitu

Scholarship Student
Tabora Rosin
(in Papua New Guinea)

United Church in Papua New Guinea

Moderator
Bernard Siai

Mission Partner
Wande Ebofin (ed)

O Love divine, to you we cry in the day and in the night, for you alone can speak to our condition. You alone can search the mind and purify the heart. You alone are infinite in love and you alone can flow over our darkness with the ocean of eternal light. O love divine, to you we cry in the day and in the night. Amen.

George Fox (1624-1691)

We give thanks for the work of John Sasabule (NMA) working as senior accountant for the Helena Goldie Hospital in the **Solomon Islands**, which is helping to ensure the hospital accounts department is run professionally so that the hospital can continue to attract the government funding it needs;
for the one-off grant from the Solomon Islands government which has enabled the hospital to clear debts and purchase important medical equipment.
We pray for the continuing work of the hospital and for the medical students, recently returned from training in Cuba.

Information supplied by the World Church Relationships Office

We pray for the women in **Papua New Guinea** to have a voice;
for their freedom from fear and violence;
for nationals of Papua New Guinea in remote places, that they may grow in confidence and take the initiative in developing projects that will help communities, and thereby the whole country, to reduce dependence on foreign intervention;
for the agency schools in Papua New Guinea, that the Church may select teachers and educational administrators wisely and responsibly.

Wande Ebofin, mission partner, Papua New Guinea

We hold in prayer all those who suffer from hidden illness.
Not every scar is visible, Lord, as yours were.
Not all pain is obvious.
We hold before you those who
are judged because people do not understand their illness,
do not behave 'normally',
self-harm,
find their illness affects every aspect of their everyday life
and for those who care for such people.
As you walk alongside them, Lord, we pray they will feel your healing touch. Amen.

Gwynn Bamford, deacon, Bromsgrove and Redditch Circuit

Traditional Pacific island welcome (Graham Longbottom)

Plymouth and Exeter District

Chair
Graham Thompson

We give thanks for a developing vision for the life of the Plymouth and Exeter District;
for the work and enthusiasm of the district's Evangelism Enabler and Safeguarding Officer;
for the development of a new diaconal appointment in Bude.
We pray for the new opportunities for mission in Clovelly, Bude and Plymouth;
for refugees living within communities in the Plymouth and Exeter District, that the people of the District may play their part in offering hospitality and support;
for ongoing and effective outreach in rural and agricultural communities.

Lord, we thank you for the freedoms that are ours.
We remember those who are trapped
by the decisions and actions of others,
as well as by themselves.
We pray for those in dark places and ask that they
may begin to see the light at the end of the tunnel,
know hope restored and freedom gained.
We ask that you grant to all the freedom
that comes from knowing Christ's transforming love
in our lives. Amen.
Graham Thompson, Plymouth and Exeter District Chair

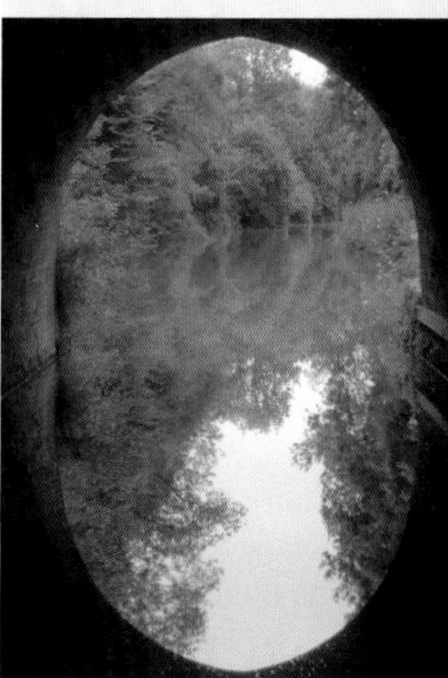
The light at the end of the tunnel (Graham Thompson)

Loving God, we give you thanks for your Church, remembering all that we share together, and look forward to everything the future holds.
We pray for your people in every place and ask for your blessing upon their lives and witness, and upon all whom you have called to service.
We pray for those involved in mission, either at home or overseas; evangelists, preachers, chaplains, mission partners and all those who proclaim the gospel and make known the love of Christ.
Loving God, guide your people, strengthen, equip and inspire each one for service, and so may we, with them, joyfully serve you, sensitively proclaim you and faithfully express your love for all.
Build up your Church, so your kingdom may come in all its fullness, through Jesus Christ our Lord. Amen.
William Mullally, President, Methodist Church in Ireland, 2016/2017

DAY 25

Praying with Christians in the Pacific

Preferring nothing to you, O Christ, let us hold fast to your love, embrace your cross and honour your name. Let conviction mark our speech, courage our life and patience our faith; for your own name's sake. Amen.

Cyprian of Carthage (c. 200-258)

Tonga

Methodist President
Finau Ahio

Samoa

Methodist President
Aisoli Iuli

Scholarship Students
Iosefa Lefaoseu (in Fiji)
Latuivai Kioa
Numerator Ofoia (both in New Zealand)

Fiji

Methodist President
Tevita Banivanua

Mission Partners
Julia Edwards (sd)
Val Ogden° (ed)

Scholarship Students
Savenaca Vuetanavanua (in Fiji)

We pray for the many refugees in parts of Asia and the Pacific who seldom feature in our news media;
for the millions who may be forced to flee their homes in low-lying regions as climate change continues to cause sea levels to rise, flooding land and making drinking water salty;
for those from coral-based islands in the Pacific who have already had to leave their homes.

Information supplied by the World Church Relationships Office

Loving eternal God of sea, earth and sky, thank you for the beautiful islands of **Tonga.**
for the Tongan people's joy at celebrating the coronation of their new King, Tupou VI, and Queen, Nanasipau'u;
for the many students training at Sia'atoutai Theological College;
for Tupou College, the oldest secondary school in the Pacific, celebrating 150 years and seeking closer ties with The Leys School.
We pray for the young people of Tonga as they face a growing invasion of Western culture and materialism;
for Tupou College, the oldest secondary school in the Pacific;
for all who work to protect the islands from the effects of climate change;
for the Tongan fellowships in Wales and London.

Stephen Poxon, minister, New River Circuit

We give thanks for the bountiful and beautiful lands of **Fiji**, and pray for all peoples to have access to just land rights;
for the commitment of political leaders, who seek justice and peace for all citizens, and pray for transparency and accountability at all levels of authority;
for the observance of the rights of the child.
We pray for justice and peace within families, as reported child-abuse cases increase;
for women and children who experience only violence and abuse, rather than love and sanctuary in the family home.

Julia Edwards, mission partner, Fiji

Portadown District (Ireland)

Superintendent
Kenneth Robinson

We give thanks for those in the Portadown District who are approaching retirement from active ministry and those probationer ministers who are starting out;
for God's grace in answers to prayer, and new forms of outreach.
We pray for the Holy Spirit of God to be revealed and share his power with us;
for many people to meet Jesus and enter a life-changing relationship;
for God's kingdom to come and bring growth in all the churches of the District.

Sheffield District

Chair
Gill Newton

We give thanks for the work of the dedicated and faithful staff of the Sheffield District as they support and resource local churches and circuits;
for the new Sunday evening 'Oasis' congregation in Victoria Hall, Sheffield;
for work among the elderly, including the creation of dementia-friendly churches.
We pray for the the covenanted area between the Sheffield Circuit and the Sheffield Anglican Diocese;
for all those leading and participating in nurture and discipleship courses across the District;
for those church communities facing challenging decisions about the way forward.

Loving God, when life is busy and the pressure is on,
it is easy to feel hemmed in by the expectations of other people
and the demands of daily living.
Yet, in Christ, you promise us freedom.
Remind me of the freedom that is to be found in knowing him.
Help me, by your Spirit,
to see beyond everything that seems to get in the way
of me being the person you made me to be
and doing the things you have for me to do.
Open my ears to the cries of all those around me,
who are denied the freedom they deserve,
and give me the courage to speak up and to speak out for them,
that all may enjoy the freedom Christ came to bring. Amen.

Gill Newton, Sheffield District Chair

See beyond everything that seems to get in the way (Sue Avery)

DAY 26

Praying with Christians in Northern Europe

The United Methodist Northern Europe and Eurasia Central Conference

Nordic and Baltic Area

Methodist Bishop
Christian Alsted

Superintendents
Denmark
Jørgen Thaarup
Keld Munk
Estonia
Taavi Hollman
Finland (Finnish and Swedish speaking)
Pasi Runonen
Mayvor Wärn-Rancken
Nils-Gustav Sahlin
Latvia
Gita Mednis
Lithuania
William Lovelace
Norway
Øyvind Helliesen
Steinar Hjerpseth
Svein Veland
Sweden
Bimbi Ollberg
Alf Englund
Thore Hildingsson

Create within us, O God, a love for your holy word. Teach us its true and inner meaning. Within its sacred pages may we find new strength and joy; by its precepts guidance for the soul, and through familiar words grace to help in time of need; for your truth and your name's sake. Amen.

Walter James (1879-1908)

We give thanks for the good and growing ecumenical co-operation with other Christian denominations in **Estonia**;
for the witness that the Ecumenical Council and Evangelical Alliance in Estonia give to the nation;
for the ministries to Estonian- and Russian-speaking people.
We pray for a strengthening in faith and holiness in believers so that there may be an increasing Christian witness in society;
for the revitalisation of older congregations and for new ministries to people who are not yet seeking God.

Taavi Hollman, Superintendent,
United Methodist Church in Estonia

We give thanks for the strengthening of ecumenical ties within **Latvia**, exemplified by one congregation opening its building to house three other denominations;
for the new Latvian Methodist hymnal which was published and dedicated in 2015.
We pray that God will send more labourers to the Latvian vineyard;
for the youth and teen ministry in the Methodist churches of Latvia as well as Camp Wesley;
for wisdom about how best to handle the refugee crisis and that the Church will be able to welcome, feed and clothe the stranger.

Gita Mednis, Superintendent,
United Methodist Church in Latvia

We give thanks for the good development of church leaders;
for work among refugees and immigrants in **Finland**;
for people who serve in different capacities.
We pray for the development of visions and plans for the Church;
for resources for planting new churches;
for dedicated Christians who will listen to God's calling.

Monica Lundgren, Lay Leader of Conference, Finland

Southampton District

Chair
Andrew Wood

The blinding light of God's presence (Steven Wild)

We give thanks for presbyteral and diaconal probationers beginning their ministry in the Southampton District;
for their insight, enthusiasm and the fresh eyes for mission which they bring to the District from their training and formation;
for willingness to take risks in the name of our God of surprises.
We pray for ecumenical partnerships with the Wessex Synod of the URC, Church of England and with the Pioneer Network in Southampton, Portsmouth and the Meon Valley;
for the ongoing mission in Tolpuddle, Dorset, and the Tolpuddle Festival in July, when many people engage with the heritage and values of Methodism at the scene of a great injustice to working people which is a sign of protest and hope for Church and trade unions;
for chaplaincies in education and healthcare across the District, particularly Portsmouth University, and major hospitals in Portsmouth, Southampton and Basingstoke, and school chaplaincies in Yeovil and Reading.

God of justice and truth, thank you for those who minister to prisoners. Strengthen those who rope themselves to prisoners with cords that cannot be broken. Help prisoners and those who support them climb towards your summit together. Open your word afresh to those who journey a lonely road, that they may be met with the blinding light of your presence. Watch over and protect the families and friends of victims and perpetrators alike; may your love shine in their lives. May we find a deeper freedom to share through facing our own truths. Amen.

Robert, prisoner, HMP Northumberland

God who is found in beauty and brokenness,
holy and gracious one,
whose heart is torn by the suffering of your children,
you long for a world of justice and plenty for all.
Liberate us to share in that freedom offered by your kingdom.
Open our eyes to sense your presence
in places of despair and fear,
open our ears to hear your call to be salt and light in the world,
melt our hearts, convert us to the needs of the other,
and move us to be your people, a people of justice and care,
for our world, for friend and stranger. Amen.

Andrew Wood, Southampton District Chair

DAY 27

Praying with Christians in Europe

Grant us, O Lord, the will to accomplish all that pleases you; the strength to do all that you command and the reverence to respect all that you have made; for your own name's sake. Amen.

Francis of Assisi (1182-1226)

The United Methodist Northern Europe and Eurasia Central Conference (cont.)

Eurasia Area

Russia

Methodist Bishop
Eduard Khegay

The United Methodist Central Conference of Germany

Methodist Bishop
Rosemarie Wenner

Mission Partners
Barry° and Gillian Sloan, Michael and Megan (p)

United Protestant Church of Belgium

President
Steven Fuite

United Protestant Church of France

President
Laurent Schlumberger

Blessed be the Lord who gives us abundant grace and mercy.
We thank you for the United Methodist Church in **Russia** and **Eurasia** and for opening new horizons for ministry and fellowship among believers of different countries.
We pray that our ways may be the paths of truth and righteousness;
for unity among the peoples of the Russian and Eurasian republics;
for wisdom, sensitivity of heart, and understanding of your will among the people of Russia and Eurasia;
for the growth of churches and for the Word of God to be made known in Russia and Eurasia;
for peace for our brothers and sisters in Ukraine.

Irina Rushkevich, fourth-year student, Moscow Theological Seminary of the United Methodist Church

We give thanks for the fresh expressions of church and new church starts that are emerging in **Germany** to serve different people with the love of God;
for the international congregations throughout Germany that reflect the unity-in-diversity that is the Body of Christ.
We pray for the local congregations who are welcoming and supporting the many refugees newly arrived in Germany;
for a successful reorientation of Church conference structures to enable an even more efficient and effective mission focus;
for the German tent mission that serves local congregations throughout Europe, equipping and enabling them to be a blessing to their neighbourhoods.

Barry and Gillian Sloan, mission partners, Germany

Dear Lord, free those who have dark lives
and brighten up their day.
Release them from the memories that haunt them. Amen.

Ethan Staley, Year 4, St Andrew's Methodist Primary School, Farnworth and Worsley Circuit

West Yorkshire District

Chair
Roger Walton

Batley Interfaith Group (© Touchstone Bradford, used with permission)

We give thanks for the pioneering mission work in Bradford, Huddersfield and Halifax;
for the developing West Yorkshire Youth Network which is helping young people to grow in their discipleship; and for all youth and children's workers across the District;
for the generous response of the churches in West Yorkshire to the floods and other tragedies hitting local communities.
We pray for the Revd Dr Barbara Glasson as she leads the District while Roger Walton serves the wider Connexion as President and for all others in the District carrying additional responsibilities this year;
for the work of Touchstone as it moves to a new base in Bradford;
for preparations for an evangelism initiative in all circuits in 2017.

Father God, we praise you for the impact of our Church in education. Thank you for the commitment of Methodist school head teachers, staff, chaplains and governors to excellence, and the creative communication of faith in Jesus and equipping children and young people for their life journeys. May many discover Jesus for themselves and serve him all their days. Bless, strengthen and guide all who teach and care in our schools, expressing your love especially to those in greatest need, and aiming to develop whole people more than A stars. Amen.

Philip Clarke, superintendent minister, Burnley Circuit

Joyous God,
 who sings the world *a capella* style,
 who improvises joy in unlikely events,
 and breathes an exuberant spirit to set the world dancing;
help us, your unlikely followers,
 to glimpse the twinkle in your creative eye
 and to see a wonderful hope in dark and chaotic places;
so that, even within sorrow and struggle, we may discover glimmers of hope,
 within pain, the possibilities of transformation;
 and within injustice, our own power to change the world for good.
Most of all, God, don't let us be dull.
Give us the courage to join your exuberant enterprise called life,
to laugh at our own impossibilities and ridiculous notions
and, in all this, to trust, that through you and in you and with your love,
we and all your people should, and can and will be free. Amen.

Barbara Glasson, West Yorkshire District Deputy Chair

DAY 28

Praying with Christians in Central Europe

Teach us, O God, to trust your providence, ordered and sure; to accept your wisdom, unerring and true; and to rejoice in your love unbounded and eternal; through Christ our Lord. Amen.

Charles Simeon (1759-1836)

United Methodist Central and Southern Europe Central Conference

Methodist Bishop
Patrick Streiff

Superintendents

Austria
Stefan Schröckenfuchs

Bulgaria, Romania
Daniel Topalski

Czech Republic
Petr Procházka

Hungary
László Khaled

Poland
Andrzej Malicki
Józef Bartos
Sławomir Rodaszyński
Waldemar Eggert

Slovakia
Pavel Procházka

Pastor Ivan Morunov and a friend making music, Bulgaria (Üllas Tankler)

We give thanks for thousands of volunteers in **Austria** (including people from Methodist congregations) who have been serving refugees from Syria, Iraq and Afghanistan;
for the hundreds of churches which have provided spaces as refugee shelters.
We pray for the UMC's work with homeless people in Vienna during the winter.

Lothar Pöll, former Superintendent, Austria

We give thanks for the growth that God has granted to the local churches since the UMC in **Romania** was started in 2011;
for the planting of a second local church, in the city of Sibiu.
We pray for the planting of new local churches in rural areas, in Roma communities and in new villages;
for the first church building of the UMC in Romania in Cluj-Napoca, the place where the United Methodist Church in Romania started.

Daniel Topalski, Superintendent, Bulgaria and Romania

We give thanks for the new community house in Alsozsolca, **Hungary**, which serves Roma people inside and outside the United Methodist congregation.
We pray for Hungarian families and for the United Methodist Summer Family Camp;
for the new superintendent of the United Methodist Church in Hungary.

István Csernák, former Superintendent, Hungary

We give thanks for the lay people and pastors proclaiming the gospel throughout **Slovakia**.
We pray for the students of the Methodist theological programme for laity, that they will be prepared and spiritually equipped for a variety of ministries in their local churches.
for the ordained elders, that they may faithfully continue church work in the face of a changing spiritual climate in Europe.

Pavel Procházka, Superintendent, Slovakia

Wolverhampton and Shrewsbury District

Chair
Rachel Parkinson

We give thanks for the Borderland Rural Chaplaincy as the team of chaplains grows and its range of work widens;
for the Bristol and West Midlands Discipleship and Ministries Learning Network, and especially for the Holy Habits programme which is now being developed for use in three circuits of the Birmingham District;
for the District's fruitful relationship with Rwanda, and the work of the Methodist Church in Rwanda.
We pray for Rachel Parkinson, the new Wolverhampton and Shrewsbury District Chair, that she may bring new ideas and new approaches that will build upon what has gone before;
for the team of people who work within the District to serve local churches and develop mission in local places.

Holy God who changes not, help us in times of change.
May we rejoice in what has gone before,
  but never live in the past.
May we live in the present
  as we serve the needy world of today.
May we have a vision for the future,
  but never put off until tomorrow what is needed today.
Holy God, help us to bring into being
your Church of the future. Amen.

John Howard,
former Wolverhampton and Shrewsbury District Chair

A woman gives her testimony of her faith in Rwanda (John Howard)

Dear God, I am sorry that I have not taken the opportunities to share my faith with others. Despite the freedom we have in this country to make known the love of the Lord Jesus, I have not been able or willing to speak out. I ask that you give us all the strength and courage to be more robust and sure of the faith that is in us, that others may know from our witness to God's unending love that true freedom comes from letting Jesus be our friend and guide in everything we say, think or do. In the name of the one whose service is perfect freedom. Amen.

Beryl Fudge, Abingdon

Lord, save us from sin and free us from devastation.
Child of sorrow, you gave us freedom and suffered the consequences rather than us. Amen.

Oliver Bennett, Year 4, St Andrew's
Methodist Primary School, Farnworth and Worsley Circuit

DAY 29

Praying with Christians in Central Europe

Lord Jesus Christ, wisdom and Word of God, dwell in our hearts, by your most Holy Spirit, that out of the abundance of our hearts our mouths may speak your praise. Amen.

Christina Rossetti (1830-1894)

United Methodist Central and Southern Europe Central Conference (cont.)

Superintendents

Algeria, Tunisia
Daniel Nussbaumer

Albania, Macedonia
Wilfried Nausner

Serbia
Ana Palik-Kunčak

Switzerland-France
Claudia Haslebacher
Jörg Niederer
Etienne Rudolph
Stefan Zürcher

Migrants in Sid, Serbia (Dragan Chulo)

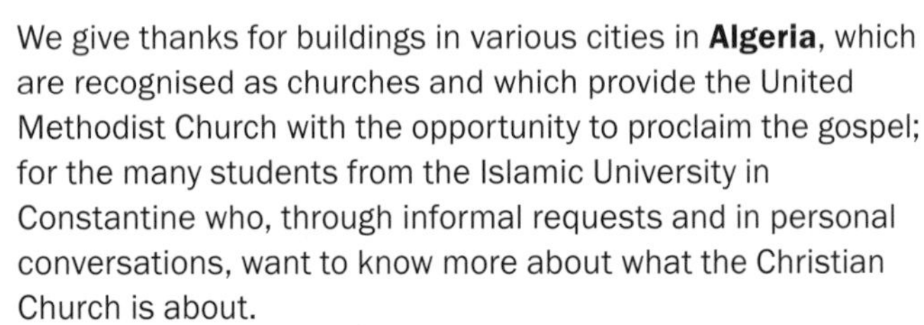

We give thanks for buildings in various cities in **Algeria**, which are recognised as churches and which provide the United Methodist Church with the opportunity to proclaim the gospel;
for the many students from the Islamic University in Constantine who, through informal requests and in personal conversations, want to know more about what the Christian Church is about.
We pray that the openness of the government towards the Christian Churches will continue so that it will remain possible to proclaim the gospel;
for newly converted Christians, that they may be strengthened to cope with their difficult situations.

Daniel Nussbaumer, Superintendent, Algeria and Tunisia

We give thanks for the work done by the Miss Stone Centre in Strumica, **Macedonia** for people who are old, homeless or disabled;
for the new church in Radovis.
We pray for the refugees that arrive daily in Macedonia and for those who serve them.

Wilfried Nausner, Superintendent, Albania and Macedonia

We give thanks for the freedom, peace and the possibility to worship and serve the Lord freely in **Serbia**.
We pray for more families to join the Church and get involved in the various ministries;
for mission and outreach projects in local churches and for the growth of their congregations.

Ana Palik-Kunčak, Superintendent, Serbia

God, the people of **Switzerland** live with so many possibilities for freedom, but they fear foreigners and what might happen. Please lead them into the freedom of your Spirit and of your love, so that they may share what they have with those in need and learn to trust in you rather than in their material securities.

Claudia Haslebacher, Superintendent, Switzerland

York and Hull District

Chair
Stephen Burgess

We give thanks that the great city of Hull has been chosen as the UK City of Culture for 2017;
for those involved in the preparations and for churches rising to the challenge of proclaiming the gospel message within the celebrations;
for strong collaboration across Yorkshire;
for the four mainly Yorkshire districts as they develop new configurations for their work.
We pray for continuing discernment in planning new ways of working within Yorkshire;
for communities recovering from the devastating floods of 2015, and for those whose homes and businesses were disrupted.

Gracious God, in your world may we continue to trust in your creating power;
where there is brokenness,
may we work with you to restore goodness for all creation.
Holy Spirit, in your Church may we continue to give thanks that you fire us up;
where there is failure,
draw us back to the community of your people, called to share the good news.
Lord Jesus, in our own lives may we trust in your everlasting presence;
when we are tempted to stray from your way,
remind us of your love for each one of us;
and at the end of this day, grant us rest and the knowledge of your presence in our lives, your Church and your world. Amen.

Stephen Burgess, York and Hull District Chair

Compassionate Jesus, you knew how it felt to be put on trial
and you charge us to care for prisoners.
We pray for those in prison,
that they may experience the good news of the gospel;
for families who travel, visit, wait, and hope,
that they might find contentment in the present;
for those who work in law enforcement or the judiciary,
that justice and mercy may be held in equal measure;
for victims of crime,
that they would be free to forgive.
Free us all from being too quick to judge,
and from putting ourselves above the need for forgiveness.
Help us to see your new way. Amen.

Pru Cahill, deacon, North Kent Circuit
and member of Prison Fellowship, Rochester

Free us all... (Sarah Small)

DAY 30

Praying with Christians in Southern Europe

God, in whom the faithful put their trust and for whom the true of heart wait in hope; guide us in the hour of perplexity, preserve us in the day of confusion and remember us in moment of our need; through Christ our Lord. Amen.

Lancelot Andrewes (1555-1626)

We give thanks for the signs of renewal in the local congregations in the Methodist Church in **Portugal** and for two new local churches started in 2015;
for all who have heard the call of God to be more involved in church life, by leading services, preaching, teaching at Sunday School, playing and singing in the praise groups and sharing the good news of Jesus in words and actions.
We pray for new candidates to the ministry and for more people to understand the importance of making a contribution, personal and financial, to the life of the Church, so that it may meet present challenges and continue to thrive.

Sifredo Teixeira, Bishop, Methodist Church in Portugal

We thank you for the work of the Church in **Spain,** which acts as a living testimony of your compassion as it opens its doors to refugees, migrants and the poor, providing them with food, counsel and company.
We pray for the Church's partner organisations: for Fraternadal (in Catalunya) and Camino (in Valencia and Alicante), which distribute food to unemployed families;
for the Bet-San foundation, working with the elderly in Barcelona;
for Prosper Acción Social Protestante in Madrid, which provides food and legal and social counselling to help facilitate integration in Spain.

Israel Folmos, Spanish Evangelical Church

We give thanks for the work of the Methodist Ecumenical Centre in Rome, **Italy**, which offers opportunities to explore better relationships with Christians of other traditions;
for the hospitality offered by Ponte Sant' Angelo Church to the thousands of pilgrims visiting Rome for the Jubilee Year of Mercy.
We pray for the Global Freedom Network, working from the faith base of the Anglican Centre in Rome, in helping to eradicate human trafficking and modern forms of slavery.

Tim Macquiban, mission partner, Rome

Portugal

Methodist Bishop
Sifredo Teixeira

Spanish Evangelical Church

President
Joel Cortés

Italy

Methodist President
TBA

Mission Partners
Tim° and Angela Macquiban (p)
Daniel° and Grace Pratt Morris-Chapman, Kwame, John and Anna (ed)

Conference of European Churches

General Secretary
Heikki Huttunen

Community of Protestant Churches in Europe

Central Secretary
Michael Bünker

Scotland District

Chair
David Easton

We give thanks for the nation of Scotland:
for the welcome from Methodist congregations to those wanting to explore or celebrate the faith and offering a welcome to those who come to minister from elsewhere;
for the opportunities presented by the opening of new premises for congregations in Anniesland and Kilsyth.
We pray for churches serving the marginalised, especially refugees and asylum seekers;
for work with students;
for the work of Action for Children;
for the community at MHA's Auchlochan Village.

Scotland has no law of trespass;
Lord, we thank you for the freedom to roam, explore and enjoy and to share with others.
God's kingdom on Earth has no law of trespass;
we thank you that you have put up the sign of the Cross that says 'all are welcome'.
The Holy Spirit has no law of trespass;
we pray, as sisters and brothers together, that we may enjoy the liberty and freedom of children of God as we live in and by the Spirit. May our inner holiness find expression in our social holiness as we share that liberty with others. Amen.

David Easton, Chair of the Methodist Church in Scotland and Shetland District

Shetland District

Chair
David Easton

Almighty and wonderful God, we thank you for the blessing and joy of freedom to worship and learn through the Methodist Church in Shetland;
for the opportunities to celebrate and share your saving grace through the weekly café at Walls, the monthly 'Pop-Up Shop' at Lerwick and Café Church at Scalloway;
for small gatherings and house groups where your word is reflected on, especially at Scalloway, Whiteness, Walls, Vidlin, East Yell and Lerwick.
We pray for the new Deputy Chair, Andrew Fox, and his wife Susie, as they settle into life in these wonderful islands;
for the church in Fair Isle and for the local preachers of Shetland as they faithfully minister in the churches of the District.

Dear Lord, I sometimes pause and think about how I would like to be. Please give shape to these thoughts, that my life may display your goodness and gracious freedom. Help me to bring you glory as I find courage through Jesus to be as you want me to be. Thank you. Amen.

Jeremy Dare, former Shetland District Chair

DAY 31

Praying with the Church around the world

Eternal God, as you have taught us to keep all your commandments by loving you and our neighbour: grant us the spirit of peace and the gift of grace, that we may be devoted to you with our whole heart and united to each other with a pure will; through Jesus Christ our Lord. Amen.

Ambrosian Missal (8th century)

God of justice and freedom, we thank you for the service for **Women's World Day of Prayer 2017*** written by the Christian women of the Philippines. It reminds us of the injustices under which many people, particularly women, are forced to live.
We dedicate ourselves to eradicate the causes of injustice that threaten human dignity.
We pray that, as you transform seeds into fruit, so you will use us to plant and nurture seeds of justice, that they may flourish and spread throughout the whole world. Amen.

Elizabeth Burroughs, Methodist representative,
National Committee for England, Wales and Northern Ireland

We pray for the **World Federation of Methodist and Uniting Church Women** as they embark on a new quinqennium under the banner of 'Chosen people, called to proclaim'. May women in every Area, Unit and local church find freedom in serving Jesus, increase their knowledge of his abiding love, and make him known in their communities, proclaiming Christ, the liberating Lord. Amen.

Alison Judd, World Federation Area Officer,
Methodist Women in Britain

Prayer for international students
We pray for those who leave their country and kindred to study in the UK. May the gifts of curiosity, creativity and intellect that you have given prepare them better to serve their communities. As they equip themselves for future ministry, so may they find hospitality and support within their communities of learning. Amen.

Samuel McBratney, Director,
Global Christianity Programme, Queen's Foundation

Mission partners and others recently returned from overseas or ending their period of service
2015/2016

Andy Dye (ed), Grenada

Ros Colwill (p), Nigeria

Glen and Wendy Lund, Julu, Kathleen, Taliesin, Tsunami (ed), Zambia [CofS is the lead agency]

Malcolm Oliver and Regina Siatwinda-Oliver, Lyando and Chipo (p/n), Mozambique

Malcolm° and Cati Ramsay (p), Nepal

Mattia Leoni and Elena Trivellato-Leoni, Michele and Sam (t/p), Rwanda

**Women's World Day of Prayer Friday 3 March 2017. The service has been written by the Christian women of the Philippines and is entitled* Am I being unfair to you?

Lord we praise you that we have the freedom to worship you, the freedom to pray to you and the freedom to share the good news of your kingdom with others. We pray for those countries where Christians have to worship in secret and pray privately due to the fear of being arrested, and cannot openly share the love of God with others. Amen.

Jean Whetham, local preacher, Falmouth and Gwennap Circuit

Loving God, who calls us to be the Body of Christ, we pray for our partnerships in Europe through the **European Methodist Council** (EMC) and the **European Methodist Youth and Children's Council** (EMYC). We pray in particular for the new secretary of the EMYC.
We give thanks for closer working, as together we support those congregations and Conferences offering hospitality, basic information, language tuition, and care to migrants and refugees. We give thanks that lives are being changed and congregations challenged to welcome newcomers and receive their gifts and graces.
We pray for insight and imagination for those preparing the next European Festival. We also pray that the celebrations and commemorations of the Reformation throughout 2017, inspired by the 500th anniversary of Martin Luther's call for the Church to reform, will be an encouragement and cause for thanksgiving and mission. Amen.

Elaine Robinson, European Methodist Council Secretary

God of all, we give thanks for those who can speak of their memories of distant lands and other cultures and open for us a window on to a wider world. Help them to tell of how our common faith can make us one with those who dwell in foreign lands. How, though drawn from far-flung parts, we can journey together in faith. Help all who confess that Jesus is Lord to share in witnessing to his love. Whatever our mother tongue, may we acknowledge our parent God and, in our coming together, may we realise that we form one family of faith, one people, journeying to you. Amen.

Wendy Kilworth-Mason,
superintendent minister, Whitehaven Circuit

World Church Relationships

Leader
David Friswell

Partnership Coordinators:
Africa
Olubunmi Olayisade
Americas and Caribbean
Sandra Lopez
Asia-Pacific
Steve Pearce
Europe
Roy Crowder

World Methodist Council (WMC)

General Secretary
Ivan Abrahams

As a member of the WMC the Methodist Church in Britain also relates to other Methodist Churches worldwide. For a full list please see the WMC website: www.worldmethodistcouncil.org

World Council of Churches (WCC)

General Secretary
Olav Fykse Tveit

The WCC is a fellowship of 349 Churches, denominations and church fellowships in more than 110 countries and territories throughout the world, representing over 560 million Christians.

Additional Resources

A Gift of Prayer, a small treasury of prayers from around the world based on the Lord's Prayer. Available in packs of 50, priced £5 (plus p&p) from Methodist Publishing, tel: 0845 017 8220 or www.methodistpublishing.org.uk.

A Word in Time, www.methodist.org.uk/bible offers commentary on the daily readings from the Prayer Handbook.

the connexion**,** a print magazine, published three times a year, that brings together inspirational stories from Methodist people worldwide, who are passionate about sharing God's love to change lives. You can sign up to receive *the connexion* at www.methodist.org.uk/theconnexion

One Mission Matters, www.methodist.org.uk/onemissionmatters, contains information, resources and stories from Britain and the World Church.

Mission Matters...in Sri Lanka, this DVD shows how we are in living partnership with people in Sri Lanka. Available from Methodist Publishing, tel: 0845 017 8220 or www.methodistpublishing.org.uk. Note: There is a packing and postage charge of £2.50 for this free item.

One Mission, a five-session course focusing on our calling to mission, praying and giving for mission, as well as what One Mission means for Methodists today. Ideal for house groups, fellowship meetings and Bible studies. Available online only at www.methodist.org.uk/one-mission-bible-study

Prayer Focus, the Prayer Handbook of the Methodist Church in Ireland available from the Methodist Church in Ireland. For more information contact the Home Mission Department at 00353 1 5580978 or hmd@irishmethodist.org

The Methodist Recorder, from your newsagent or 122 Golden Lane, London EC1Y 0TL.

The Prayer Handbook on CD, from Galloway's Society for the Blind, Howick House, Howick Park Avenue, Penwortham, Preston PR1 0LS, tel: 01772 744148.

World Church News, sign up through www.methodist.org.uk/signup, to receive a monthly newsletter packed with news from overseas partners, mission partners and more. You can sign up to other Methodist Church email newsletters here.

Key – the letters beside the names indicate the type of work in which mission partners are mainly engaged:

- ad administration
- d doctor
- ed education
- m medical work (other than doctor or nurse)
- n nurse
- p pastoral worker
- sd social/development work
- th theological training
- ° minister
- **+ Joint Appointment**
- CMS Church Mission Society (Anglican)
- CofS Church of Scotland
- CWM Council for World Mission

Other Abbreviations

- CSFC Church of Scotland and Free Church (Chaplains)
- SALT Scholarship and Leadership Training
- WCR World Church Relationships
- UMC United Methodist Church
- MHA Methodist Homes for the Aged